Easy-Prep Lessons

Dive In!

Fun Faith-Builders

David C Cook®

transforming lives together

DIVE IN!
Published by David C. Cook
4050 Lee Vance View
Colorado Springs, CO 80918 U.S.A.

David C. Cook Distribution Canada
55 Woodslee Avenue, Paris, Ontario, Canada N3L 3E5

David C. Cook U.K., Kingsway Communications
Eastbourne, East Sussex BN23 6NT, England

Written by Jodi Hoch
Cover Design: BMB Design/ScottJohnson
Cover Photos: © Gaylon Wampler Photography
Interior Design: Sandy Flewelling
Illustrations: Kris and Sharon Cartwright

ISBN 978-1-4347-6693-9

First Printing 2008
Printed in the United States

5 6 7 8 9 10 11 12 13 14

020112

David C Cook
transforming lives together

TABLE OF CONTENTS

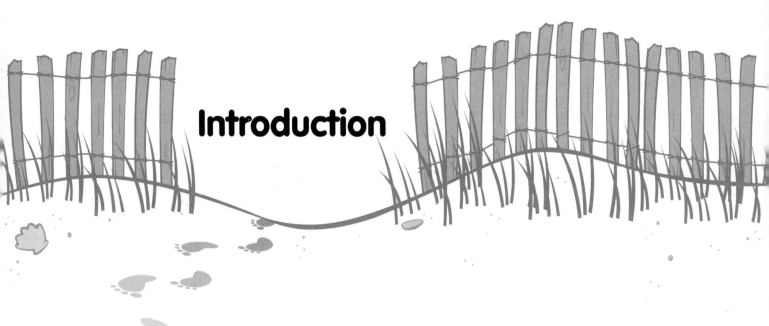

Introduction

Ready ... set ... dive in! As a teacher of young children you need to keep your little ones busy and active. Well, dive in ... to a resource that is flooded with ideas designed to keep your little ones busy, yet drenched in the Word of God. Young children are like little sponges just waiting to soak up anything you are willing to splash at them. As their teacher, you have been given the opportunity, the privilege and the challenge to make an eternal impression on the lives of the children you teach. So where do you begin?

Dive In! Easy-prep Lessons for Ages Three through Five will provide you with 13 exciting lessons packed with activities to draw young children into fun, creative and meaningful learning. Each lesson is designed for flexibility. A lesson could be completed in one hour or stretched over a longer period of time, depending on the activities you choose. Each lesson is designed for grouping flexibility and personal teaching preferences. *Dive In!* contains ideas for large groups, small groups, individuals or activity stations—adapt it to suit your classroom needs.

Dive In! is filled with Bible stories that engage the children in the telling of the Bible story. A *Flippers Up* reproducible page tailored to each lesson gives the children a hands-on creation of their own to augment their participation in telling the Bible story.

We know how a *Home Connection* that links what has been learned in the classroom with daily experiences at home helps strengthen the learning. *Dive In!* uses materials that are commonly found in a home. When the child sees something used during class, such as a cotton ball, a home connection is made to the Bible story. *Home Connection* is a reproducible page with information about the lesson for the parent. It gives parents simple at-home activities that tie in with those used in the lesson.

Dive In! equips you to meet social, developmental and spiritual needs of the youngsters in your classroom. Children will begin a voyage that is sure to excite them and touch their lives in an amazing way.

So dive in for a great adventure!

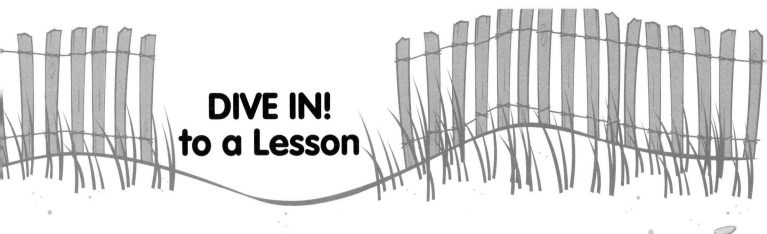

DIVE IN!
to a Lesson

Dive In! adapts to meet your classroom needs. Listed here are the basic parts of each lesson. Select and sequence these components to create your own lessons based on your preferences, time frame, number of helpers you have and the needs of your students.

Lesson Snapshot: This convenient chart at the start of each lesson shows all of the items you will need to complete each activity of that lesson.

Flippers Up: Use the reproducible page and the items listed to help the children create their *Flippers Up*. These are used with the Bible story so they must be completed **before** Bible Story Time. Each page requires about five to ten minutes to complete.

Splash-n-Spray: There are three *Splash-n-Spray* activities for each lesson: a Bible Story Link, a game and an extension activity. Each activity takes approximately five to ten minutes. Use these **anytime** during the lesson to splash a connection between concepts covered in the Bible story, to build experience in the children's everyday lives or to spray some knowledge related to concepts taught in the lesson.

Soak It In Bible Story Activities: There are three activities for each lesson: a snack, a Bible memory activity and a busy hands activity. You may choose to do these activities **anytime** during the lesson. They may be set up as activity centers or completed together in a guided project. If you choose to do these activities before the Bible story, the activities lay a foundation of experiences with concepts that will be taught later on. If done after the Bible story, these activities help to soak in and reinforce the concepts that were just taught.

Sail Away: Each lesson has three *Sail Away* activities to use **after** the Bible Story Time and just before the children leave. One activity quickly reviews the Bible story and ends with a prayer. There is also an interactive idea to help with cleanup time. As the children leave, the Homeward Bound activity suggests an idea to leave them with a concrete and tangible connection to the Bible story.

Home Connection: This is a reproducible for the parent that is sent home with the children. If you use the material from one lesson over two or three weeks, send the *Home Connection* on the last day you present the lesson.

Lesson 1

THE GREATEST GIFT (CHRISTMAS)

Bible Story: Matthew 2:1–12

Bible Truth: Jesus is God's greatest gift.

Bible Verse: For God so loved the world that he gave his one and only Son. (John 3:16a)

Children are full of wonder and excitement at Christmastime because its a season of celebrations, special events, family gatherings and giving. May your youngsters be full of joy as you introduce them to and help them celebrate the greatest gift of all—Jesus.

- In this lesson children will **hear** the story of how the wise men followed a star to find Jesus.

- In this lesson children will **learn** that Jesus is the greatest gift God has given to us.

- In this lesson children will **remember** we can be full of joy because God gave us the best gift of all—Jesus.

LESSON ONE SNAPSHOT

Flippers Up
Reproducible Page

- [ ] 1 copy of the *Flippers Up* reproducible on page 9 for each child
- [ ] Wrapping paper
- [ ] Scissors
- [ ] Crayons or markers
- [ ] Glue sticks

Splash-n-Spray

Bible Story Link:
It's a Wrap!
- [ ] Empty box
- [ ] Plain wrapping paper
- [ ] Tape
- [ ] Permanent marker

Game: *Star Light*
- [ ] Construction paper
- [ ] Scissors
- [ ] Tape
- [ ] Flashlight
- [ ] Chair

Extension Activity:
A Joy-Full Gift
- [ ] Balloons
- [ ] String or yarn
- [ ] Individually wrapped bite-size candy

Soak It In
Bible Story
Hands-on Activities

Activity 1:
Star Bites
- [ ] Cheese slices
- [ ] Triangular-shaped crackers
- [ ] Paper plates
- [ ] Small cups

Activity 2:
A Great Gift
- [ ] 1 small wrapped box
- [ ] 1 medium wrapped box
- [ ] 1 large wrapped box
- [ ] Marker

Activity 3:
A Starry Gift
- [ ] Cardstock
- [ ] Scissors
- [ ] Christmas wrapping paper
- [ ] Glue
- [ ] Water
- [ ] Bowls or cups
- [ ] Cotton swabs
- [ ] Hole punch
- [ ] Yarn

Bible Story Time
- [ ] Bible
- [ ] Completed *Flippers Up* made from the reproducible page

Sail Away

Prayer
- [ ] Basket
- [ ] Ribbon
- [ ] Scissors

Cleanup
- [ ] None

Homeward Bound
- [ ] Completed *Flippers Up*
- [ ] Small stick-on gift bow for each child
- [ ] Copy of *Home Connection* from page 14 for each child

HEART OF THE STORY

This is an amazing story of how the King of all kings was discovered by the rest of the world. The Jews were not the only ones who were awaiting a new king or Messiah. The wise men, leaders from most likely Persia or southern Arabia, were anxiously awaiting a new king as well. The star in the sky was an indication that the one to inherit Israel's throne was born with astrological importance. Immediately these Gentiles began their journey to see the greatest gift ever given to the world—Jesus.

Flippers Up
Bible Story Reproducible Page

Get List:
- A copy of the reproducibles on this page for each child
- Wrapping paper
- Scissors
- Crayons or markers
- Glue sticks

Copy the star and smaller pieces for each child. Have the children color the pictures then cut them out. Cut out the large star. Glue the small pieces onto the star as indicated. Cut a 2" by 3" piece of wrapping paper for each child. Have the children glue that as a flap over baby Jesus.

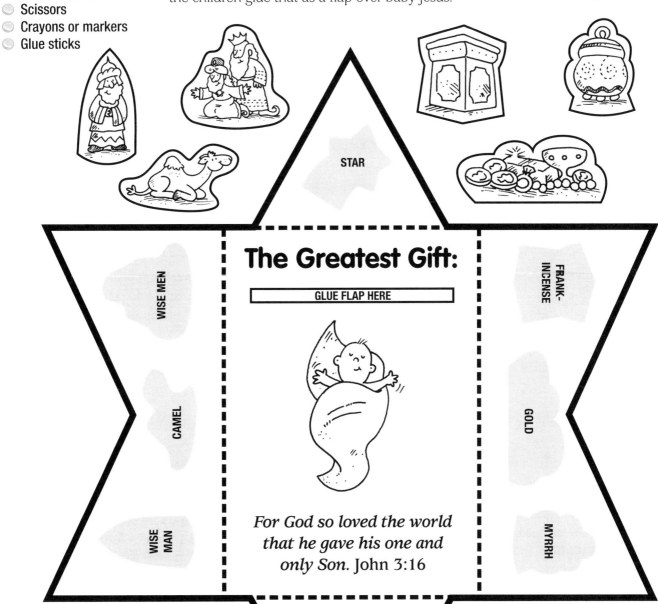

STAR

The Greatest Gift:

GLUE FLAP HERE

For God so loved the world that he gave his one and only Son. John 3:16

WISE MEN

CAMEL

WISE MAN

FRANK-INCENSE

GOLD

MYRRH

BETHLEHEM

Splash-n-Spray

Use these *Splash-n-Spray* activities to build knowledge that enriches the children's experience with the lesson while having fun.

Get List:
- Empty box
- Plain wrapping paper
- Tape
- Permanent marker

Bible Story Link

It's a Wrap!

Before class, wrap an empty box with plain wrapping paper as a gift. Have the children sit around the wrapped gift box. Pass the wrapped box around as the group joins together in this simple rap: **A gift for me, a gift for you, the greatest gift, oh it is true.** When the rap comes to an end, the child holding the gift tells about the best gift he or she has ever received. Write the gift item mentioned on the side of the gift box. Continue until all children have had a turn.

Get List:
- Construction paper
- Scissors
- Tape
- Flashlight
- Chair

Game

Star Light

Cut large stars from construction paper. Make twice as many stars as you have children. Space stars in large steps on the floor in a long continuous path. Tape each star so it won't slide. Have each child stand on a star. You stand on a chair in the corner of the playing area. Children jump or step in one direction from star to star as you say **Star light, star bright, move <u>three</u> stars tonight.** The children count each step as they travel three stars. When they stop, shine your light on a child's star and ask that child how many stars they should travel the next night to find baby Jesus. Repeat, substituting the suggested number. Continue several times around your path.

Get List:
- Balloons
- String or yarn
- Individually wrapped bite-size candy

Extension Activity

A Joy-Full Gift

Give each child a balloon and a piece of bite-size candy. **Jesus is the sweetest gift. Do you know someone who needs the sweet gift of Jesus? Let's give a friend or family member a sweet gift to remind them of the sweet gift of Jesus.** Have each child push the piece of candy inside the balloon. Remind students that Jesus fills us with joy just as the balloons are filled with air. After blowing up the balloons, help children to hold on to them while you attach a piece of string or yarn. Remind them to give their gift to someone with whom they can share the sweet gift of Jesus, who fills us with joy.

Soak It In
Bible Story Hands-on Activities

These activities can be used with large or small groups or as individual stations.

Get List:
- Cheese slices
- Triangular-shaped crackers
- Paper plates
- Small cups

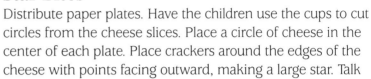

Star Bites

Distribute paper plates. Have the children use the cups to cut circles from the cheese slices. Place a circle of cheese in the center of each plate. Place crackers around the edges of the cheese with points facing outward, making a large star. Talk with the children about when and where they can see stars, and how wise men saw a star in the sky that led them to Jesus. *Note: Check with parents for food allergies.*

Get List:
- 1 small wrapped box
- 1 medium wrapped box
- 1 large wrapped box
- Marker

Activity 2

A Great Gift

For God so loved the world that he gave his one and only Son. (John 3:16a)

On the large wrapped box write, "For God so loved the world." On the medium box write, "He gave his one and only." On the small box write "Son. John 3:16." Have the children stack the boxes as they say the parts of the Bible Verse. You might run a relay with the boxes. Stack boxes at one end of the room. A teammate runs to get the first box and bring it back to the team. The next player runs to get the second box, and so on. Once all the boxes are stacked, the team shouts the verse together. Repeat until everyone has had a turn or you have rerun the relay with variations such as hop on one foot and so on.

Get List:
- Cardstock
- Scissors
- Christmas wrapping paper
- Glue
- Water
- Bowls or cups
- Cotton swabs
- Hole punch
- Yarn

A Starry Gift

Cut a large star from cardstock for each child. Let the children cut or tear small pieces of Christmas wrapping paper. Mix glue and water in equal proportions in bowls or cups so it can be spread easily with cotton swabs. Let the children dip cotton swabs in the dilluted glue to spread it on their stars. Place wrapping paper pieces onto the stars. Punch a hole in the top of the star and loop a piece of yarn through the hole. Talk about how God put a star in the sky to show the wise men where to find God's greatest gift—Jesus.

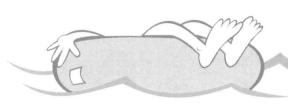

Soak It In
Bible Story Time

Get List:
- Bible
- Completed *Flippers Up* made from the reproducible page

Gather the children for story time. Be sure each one has a *Flippers Up* ready to go. Hold up a Bible for the children to see.

The book of Matthew in the Bible tells us about a journey that some really important men, called the wise men, took a long time ago. These men used to study the stars at night. Did I say the word *star?* What are you holding in your laps? Wait for response. That's right—a star. Whenever you hear me say <u>star,</u> hold up your stars and then put them back in your laps. Let's give it a try.

The wise men looked in the night skies at the <u>stars</u>. One night they noticed a very special <u>star</u>. This was no ordinary <u>star</u>. This was a <u>star</u> that would lead the wise men to a newborn baby King. The newborn baby King was Jesus. Jesus was born in Bethlehem. Many people had been waiting for King Jesus to be born. Jesus was God's special gift to the world. He was such a special gift that God put a <u>star</u> in the sky to tell everyone he had arrived.

The <u>star</u> that was shining in the night would lead the wise men to the newborn King. So the wise men started their journey. They followed the <u>star</u> that was in the night sky. After a long journey, the <u>star</u> led them right to the house where Jesus was staying. When the wise men saw Jesus they were so happy. They had brought three special gifts to give to Jesus—gold, frankincense and myrrh. God gave us a special gift too. He gave us Jesus. **Jesus is the greatest gift anyone could have.** Show the children how they can fold their stars into nice little gifts.

- How did the wise men know that Jesus was born? *(they saw a bright shining star)*
- Who was born a baby King? *(Jesus)*
- What is the greatest gift you have ever received? *(Jesus)*

Sail Away

Get List:
- Basket
- Ribbon
- Scissors

Prayer

Cut six-inch ribbons into a basket. Pass the basket and ask each child to take a ribbon and tell about something from the Bible story. Then lead the children in this prayer: **Dear Jesus, we are so happy you are our special gift from God. Thank you for being our special King. You fill our hearts with joy. In Jesus' name, amen.**

Get List:
- None

Cleanup

The wise men gave Jesus three gifts. As the children clean up, have them link arms together in groups of three. Have them pretend they are the three special gifts that Jesus received. You might even call them by their new names—Gold, Frank and Myrrh.

Get List:
- Completed *Flippers Up*
- Small stick-on gift bow for each child
- Copy of *Home Connection* for each child

Homeward Bound

As the children leave, make sure they have their completed *Flippers Up* they made for Bible Story Time and the *Home Connection* from page 14. Show them how to fold the *Flippers Up* into a gift and give each child a small gift bow to stick on the top. Tell them the bow reminds you of the greatest gift God has given us—Jesus. Be sure each child has a *Home Connection* to take home.

- What does this bow remind you of?
- Who is God's greatest gift?

PINT-SIZE BIBLE BITES

The Magi traveled a great distance to find the Christ child. Jesus was probably one or two years old when the Magi finally encountered him.

TEACHER TIP

If a child uses a *Flippers Up* or other learning object to annoy a neighbor, ask that child to show how you have said the object should be used. If needed, offer a choice to use the object as instructed or let you keep it until classtime ends.

Home Connection
Dive In!

Title: The Greatest Gift (Christmas)

Bible Story: Matthew 2:1-12

Bible Truth: Jesus is God's greatest gift.

Bible Verse: For God so loved the world that he gave his one and only Son. (John 3:16a)

○ In this lesson your child **heard** the story of how the wise men followed a star to find Jesus.

○ In this lesson your child **learned** that Jesus is the greatest gift God has given to us.

○ In this lesson your child **remembered** we can be full of joy because God gave us the best gift of all—Jesus.

When the wise men saw the star in the sky they knew the new Israelite King had been born. They followed the star all the way to Bethlehem. When they found Jesus they worshipped him and gave him gifts. Unwrap the truth this season as you help your child to see the most important gift we could ever receive—Jesus.

HOME CONNECTIONS

These are items used during the Bible story lesson that might be commonly found in your home. When your child sees or plays with one of the items mentioned below, help make the connection to the Bible story.

Star: A star was used throughout the lesson to represent the star that the wise men followed to find Jesus. When you see a star in the sky remind your child of the wise men and how they followed a star to find Jesus.

Gifts and bows: During class the children played games with gifts and did activities with bows. When these items are used at home, help your child remember the greatest gift of all—Jesus.

Flashlight: The children played a game with a flashlight. When you use a flashlight, remind your child of the star that shone bright at night that led the wise men to find Jesus.

KEEPING CONNECTED

Here are two simple activities and a prayer that were used in class during the Bible story lesson: The Greatest Gift. Use these activities to help your child remember the Bible story lesson.

Star Bites

Have your child use a cup to cut circles from cheese slices. Place a circle of cheese in the center of a plate. Place triangular-shaped crackers around the edges of the cheese with points facing outward, making a large star. Discuss with your child when he or she can see stars, and how a long time ago wise men saw a star in the sky that led them to Jesus.

A Great Gift

Use three different sized gift boxes. As you stack them one on top of the other, say the Bible Verse with your child. As you place the first box down say, **"For God so loved the world."** Then place the second box on top of the first box, saying, **"He gave his one and only…"** Finally, place the last box on top of the stack and shout, **"Son!"**

Prayer

As you tuck your little one in bed tonight, take a minute to look out the window and look at the stars. Talk about the stars God made. Talk about a special star that God made a long time ago. The special star told everyone about a very special baby who had been born—Jesus. Then pray this prayer together: **Dear God, thank you for the stars in the sky. Thank you for the greatest gift you gave to us— Jesus. In Jesus' name, amen.**

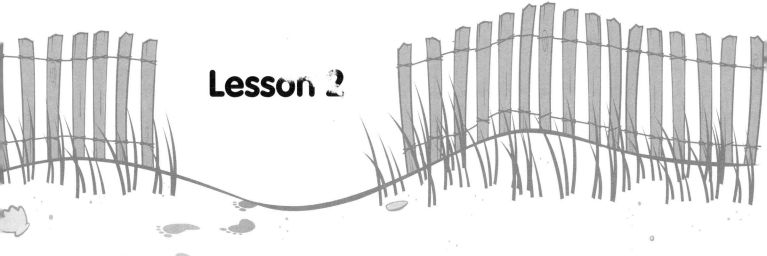

Lesson 2

HE'S NOT HERE! (EASTER)

Bible Story: Mark 16:1–8

Bible Truth: He has risen. Jesus is alive.

Bible Verse: I tell you the truth, he who believes has everlasting life. (John 6:47)

H ave a hopping good time with the children as you help them learn about the events and meaning of Easter. Understanding the miraculous events connected with the death and resurrection of Jesus help lead us to faith, hope and joy in Jesus. Join the children in focusing on and celebrating the truth— Jesus is alive! He has risen!

- In this lesson children will **hear** the story of how the stone was rolled away from the tomb.

- In this lesson children will **learn** that Jesus did not stay dead; he has risen and is alive.

- In this lesson children will **remember** to be happy because Jesus is alive. Jesus lives today.

LESSON TWO SNAPSHOT

Flippers Up
Reproducible Page

- [ ] 1 copy of the *Flippers Up* reproducible on page 17 for each child
- [ ] Scissors
- [ ] Hole Punch
- [ ] Glue
- [ ] Toothpicks
- [ ] Whole cloves
- [ ] Ground cinnamon
- [ ] Oat rings cereal
- [ ] Metal brads

Splash-n-Spray

Bible Story Link: *The Wave*
- [ ] Large piece of construction paper
- [ ] Scissors
- [ ] Marker
- [ ] Tape
- [ ] Large craft stick

Game: *Roll Away*
- [ ] Masking tape
- [ ] 10 or more foam balls
- [ ] 5 paper plates

Extension Activity:
Celebration Song
- [ ] Optional: Rhythm instruments

Soak It In
Bible Story
Hands-on Activities

Activity 1:
Empty Cross
- [ ] Fruit leather
- [ ] Oat rings cereal
- [ ] Paper plates

Activity 2:
Stepping Stones
- [ ] 12 large sheets of construction paper
- [ ] Scissors
- [ ] Tape

Activity 3:
Stone Art
- [ ] Various colors tempera paint
- [ ] Paint brushes
- [ ] Rocks of various sizes and shapes
- [ ] Glue
- [ ] Paper plates

Bible Story Time
- [ ] Bible
- [ ] Completed *Flippers Up* made from the reproducible page

Sail Away

Prayer
- [ ] Stone

Cleanup
- [ ] None

Homeward Bound
- [ ] Completed *Flippers Up*
- [ ] Oat rings cereal, one piece per child
- [ ] Copy of *Home Connection* from page 22 for each child

HEART OF THE STORY

Is it possible for someone to be dead and then come to life again? A person can when the power of God is involved! Jesus is the Son of God, and we have proof he was raised from the dead because of the empty tomb. The stone was rolled away so everyone could see the tomb was empty. Jesus was not in the tomb—he had risen from the dead just as he said he would. Not a stone, nor a Roman seal, nor a Roman guard could keep Jesus in the grave. Rejoice with your youngsters as you declare together Jesus is not dead. The stone has been rolled away. He is not in the tomb. He has risen, and he is alive!

Flippers Up
Bible Story Reproducible Page

Get List:
- A copy of the reproducible on this page for each child
- Scissors
- Hole punch
- Glue
- Toothpicks
- Whole cloves
- Ground cinnamon
- Oat rings cereal
- Metal brads

Copy and cut out the three circles for each child. Punch a hole in each where indicated. Have the children glue toothpicks to the cross, whole cloves and ground cinnamon on the tomb and cereal to the stone. Attach the three circles together in order from smallest to largest using a metal brad.

He has risen. Jesus is alive!

He's not here.

The stone was rolled away.

Splash-n-Spray

Use these *Splash-n-Spray* activities to build knowledge that enriches the children's experience with the lesson while having fun.

The Wave

Get List:
- Large piece of construction paper
- Scissors
- Marker
- Tape
- Large craft stick

Bible Story Link

Cut out a large heart. Draw a happy face on one side and a sad face on the other. Tape the bottom of the heart to a large craft stick. Have all the children sit in a long row. Start by standing at one end of the row with the sad face showing. **In today's Bible story, you're going to learn that people's hearts were sad because Jesus died. But then the people found out Jesus was alive, and their hearts became happy.** Turn the heart to the happy face then run down the row. As you run, have the children do the wave. Then have them take turns telling about times when their hearts were sad but then turned happy, so they can do the wave too.

Roll Away

Get List:
- Masking tape
- 10 or more foam balls
- 5 paper plates

Game

Use masking tape to make a large circle on the floor. Spread out five plates in the circle. Place a ball on each plate. **Today you'll hear in our Bible story how a stone was rolled away. Stand outside the circle and throw a ball to roll a stone (ball) off a plate. When you cause a stone to roll off, shout out, "Roll the stone away, for Jesus has risen today!"** Players may go into the circle to retrieve the ball but must step outside the circle to throw a ball at the targets.

Celebration Song

Get List:
- Optional: Rhythm instruments

Extension Activity

Have the children gather in a circle to sing this song to the tune of *Skip to My Lou*. Kids will enjoy clapping their hands or stomping their feet to the beat, or using rhythm instruments as they sing. On the second verse, kids can jump up when singing, "risen from the grave."

Everybody clap and sing. (3x)
The stone is rolled away.

Jesus died but rose again. (3x)
He's risen from the grave!

Soak It In
Bible Story Hands-on Activities

These activities can be used with large or small groups or as individual stations.

Get List:
- Fruit leather
- Oat rings cereal
- Paper plates

Activity 1

Empty Cross

Give each child a plate and two strips of fruit leather. Have the children make a cross using fruit leather. **Jesus died on the cross. Then he was buried in a tomb with a large stone covering the tomb. Cover your crosses with little cereal "stones".** The stone was rolled away. Jesus was not dead. He is alive! Have them eat the "stones" or roll them off of the cross. **The empty cross is a reminder that Jesus has risen and he is alive today.** *Note: Check with parents for food allergies.*

Get List:
- 12 large sheets of construction paper
- Scissors
- Tape

Activity 2

Stepping Stones

I tell you the truth, he who believes has everlasting life. (John 6:47)

Cut 12 large stone shapes from construction paper. Tape the stones in a row on the floor about six inches apart. Line up the children behind you at the first stone. Say the Bible Verse and reference together taking a step at each word as you walk down your stone path. Talk about how the stone over Jesus' tomb rolled away because Jesus rose from the dead. Lead the children back down the stone path going the other direction as you repeat the verse.

Get List:
- Various colors tempera paint
- Paint brushes
- Rocks of various sizes and shapes
- Glue
- Paper plates

Activity 3

Stone Art

Have the children glue stones onto paper plates in the shape of a cross. They can then decorate or paint their stones. Explain how their stone crosses can remind us of how Jesus died and of the stone that was rolled away because Jesus did not stay in the tomb. We know Jesus is alive.

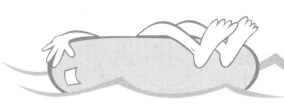

Soak It In
Bible Story Time

Get List:
- Bible
- Completed *Flippers Up* made from the reproducible page

Gather the children for story time. Be sure they have their *Flippers Up* ready to go. Hold up a Bible for the children to see.

In the Bible in the book of Mark, we learn about a story that started out sad and then ended up happy. At first everyone was sad because Jesus died on a cross. Everyone show me the picture of your cross. Have the children show you the pictures of their crosses. **Who died on the cross?** *(Jesus)* **That's right—Jesus died on the cross.**

After Jesus died on the cross, he was buried in a tomb. Everyone show me the picture of your tomb. Have the children show you their pictures. **A tomb is a cave that is used as a grave. It is where Jesus was laid after he died. Some Roman soldiers rolled a very large stone in front of the opening to the tomb so no one could get in or out of the tomb. Show me your stone in front of the tomb.** Have the children move their stone in front of their tombs.

One morning some women went to visit Jesus' tomb. The women loved Jesus, and they were very sad that he was dead. They brought spices to Jesus' tomb. When they arrived at the tomb they were shocked by what they saw. Do you know what they saw? Using your story pictures show me what they saw. Have the children move the stone away from the tomb. **They saw the stone was rolled away. The tomb was empty.**

When the women looked inside the tomb, do you know what they saw? They saw an angel dressed in white. The angel told the women not to be sad because Jesus was not dead. He was alive. Jesus was not in the grave. The women were so happy to know that Jesus was alive. We can be happy too. We know that Jesus has risen. Jesus is alive.

- **Who died, but is now alive?** *(Jesus)*
- **How do we know that Jesus is alive?** *(his tomb is empty)*

Sail Away

Get List:
- Stone

Prayer

Have the children sit in a circle. Pass a stone around the circle. As you pass the stone have them say with you, "Roll the stone away, Jesus is alive today." The person holding the stone when you say, "today," tells one thing he or she remembers from the Bible story. When everyone has had a turn, end with this prayer: **Dear God, we are so happy Jesus is alive today. Help us to tell others so everyone will know Jesus is alive. We love you. In Jesus' name, amen.**

Get List:
- None

Cleanup

As the children are cleaning up, repeat the following phrase: "The stone was rolled away, Jesus is alive … Hurray!" Have the children shout together, "Hurray!" then jump up. Keep repeating the phrase and having the children shout and jump as they clean. The faster you say the phrase, the more fun they will have.

Get List:
- Completed *Flippers Up*
- Oat rings cereal, one piece per child
- Copy of *Home Connection* for each child

Homeward Bound

As the children leave, make sure they have their completed *Flippers Up* they made for Bible Story Time and the *Home Connection* from page 22. Ask each child to show you and tell you about one of the pictures from their *Flippers Up*. Then hand each child a piece of cereal. Tell them a little round stone reminds you of the stone that was rolled away, because Jesus is alive today!

- What does the stone remind you of?
- Who died but is now alive?

PINT-SIZE BIBLE BITES

Bringing spices to a grave was an act of devotion and love very similar to today's practice of placing flowers on a grave.

TEACHER TIP

Some children may be shy or a little uncomfortable in a class setting. As a result, they might need time to sit back and see what is going on before they join an activity. Continue to invite any children who are reluctant to join in. Ask if there is anything you can do to help. If asked, parents might suggest ways to get their children involved.

Home Connection
Dive In!

Title: He's Not Here! (Easter)

Bible Story: Mark 16:1–8

Bible Truth: He has risen. Jesus is alive.

Bible Verse: I tell you the truth, he who believes has everlasting life. (John 6:47)

- In this lesson your child **heard** the story of how the stone was rolled away from the tomb.

- In this lesson your child **learned** that Jesus did not stay dead; he has risen and is alive.

- In this lesson your child **remembered** that we should be happy because Jesus is alive. Jesus lives today.

How sad and distraught we are when we discover someone has died. Jesus died long ago, and people were truly sad. The women in this Bible story went to the tomb to show their love for Jesus and dedication to him. How amazed they must have been to discover the stone had been rolled away and Jesus was not there. Jesus was alive! He had risen from the dead just as he had said. Explain your joy from knowing Jesus is alive with your child.

HOME CONNECTIONS

These are items used during the Bible story lesson that might be commonly found in your home. When your child sees or plays with one of the items mentioned below, help make the connection to the Bible story.

Stones and round cereal: Throughout the lesson, stones and round oat cereal were used as reminders of the great stone that was rolled in front of Jesus' tomb. The stone was rolled away, revealing that Jesus had risen from the dead. Whenever you see a stone remind your child of the stone that was rolled away because Jesus is alive.

Cloves and cinnamon: These spices were used in the lesson as a reminder of the spices that were brought to Jesus' tomb. When these spices are used at home, remember the wonderful surprise the ladies witnessed at the empty tomb.

KEEPING CONNECTED

Here are two simple activities from today's Bible lesson: He's Not Here! Use these activities to help your child remember the Bible story lesson.

Stepping Stones

Draw 12 stones on the sidewalk with chalk. Say the Bible Verse as you and your child jump from stone to stone. Talk about how the stones remind you of the stone at Jesus' tomb that was rolled away. Because the stone was rolled away we know that the tomb was empty. The tomb is empty because Jesus has risen. He is alive.

Empty Cross

Have your child make a cross from two strips of fruit leather. Explain how Jesus died on the cross and was buried in a tomb with a large stone covering the opening. Tell your child to cover the cross with little "stones" (cereal). Then eat the "stones" or roll them off the cross, symbolizing how the stone rolled away.

Prayer

Tell your child about a time when you were sad, but then your sadness turned to happiness. Talk about how, in the Bible story, the women were sad at first because Jesus had died but then were happy to find out he had risen and was alive. Then pray this prayer together: **Dear God, we know there will always be both sad and happy times in our lives. I am so happy Jesus rose again. I love you. In Jesus' name, amen.**

Lesson 3

GREAT LOVE
(VALENTINE'S DAY)

Bible Story: Ruth 1—4

Bible Truth: God wants us to love and care for others.

Bible Verse: Be strong and take heart, all you who hope in the LORD. (Psalm 31:24)

Young children have a natural tendency to willingly and unselfishly show others love and kindness. Foster this natural desire as you teach your youngsters how God can do amazing things when we spread his love to others.

- In this lesson children will **hear** the story of how Ruth loved and cared for Naomi.

- In this lesson children will **learn** that the love and care we show others can make them happy.

- In this lesson children will **remember** that God wants us to show love and care to others.

LESSON THREE SNAPSHOT

Flippers Up
Reproducible Page

- ☐ 1 copy of the *Flippers Up* reproducible on page 25 for each child
- ☐ Glue
- ☐ Brown yarn
- ☐ Markers or crayons
- ☐ Scissors
- ☐ Tape

Splash-n-Spray

Bible Story Link:
Gathering Grain
- ☐ Index cards
- ☐ Scissors
- ☐ Marker
- ☐ Basket

Game:
Naomi, Naomi, Ruth!
- ☐ None

Extension Activity:
Ribbons of Love
- ☐ Different colored rolls of streamers

Soak It In
Bible Story
Hands-on Activities

Activity 1:
Spreading Love
- ☐ Small tortillas
- ☐ Paper plates
- ☐ Jelly
- ☐ Craft sticks
- ☐ Napkins

Activity 2:
Basket Toss
- ☐ 4 baskets
- ☐ 4 or more beanbags
- ☐ 4 pieces of paper
- ☐ Masking tape
- ☐ Marker

Activity 3:
Stick It to Others
- ☐ Cardstock
- ☐ Scissors
- ☐ Marker
- ☐ Whole grain cereal
- ☐ Glue

Bible Story Time
- ☐ Bible
- ☐ Completed *Flippers Up* baskets made from the reproducible on page 25
- ☐ Story strip pictures from the reproducible page

Sail Away

Prayer
- ☐ Basket
- ☐ Paper
- ☐ Scissors
- ☐ Marker

Cleanup
- ☐ Large baskets

Homeward Bound
- ☐ Completed *Flippers Up*
- ☐ Basket full of hearts with names on them
- ☐ Copy of *Home Connection* from page 30 for each child

HEART OF THE STORY

The story of Ruth and Naomi is one where we see love and care that truly carries us through times of great despair. Naomi's love for God spilled out onto those around her. In fact, Ruth was so drawn to Naomi that she left her family and homeland to stay with her. Both women tragically lost their husbands and faced dire circumstances as widows with no one to provide for them. But God helped them rebuild their lives and turned their sorrow to joy. The plans God has for us are always greater than anything we could imagine—just as seen in today's story. As you teach today's Bible story, remember to share with your students that God's love rebuilds and transforms lives.

Flippers Up
Bible Story Reproducible Page

Reproduce and cut out the basket and story strip for each child. Have the children color the pictures on the story strip. Let them know they may not end up with the pictures they're coloring but coloring it as a gift will show love and care toward others. Collect the story strips, cut them apart, and separate them into piles according to the numbers on the pictures. Save them for Bible Story Time. Then have the children color and glue brown yarn onto their baskets. Fold the baskets, and tape the sides.

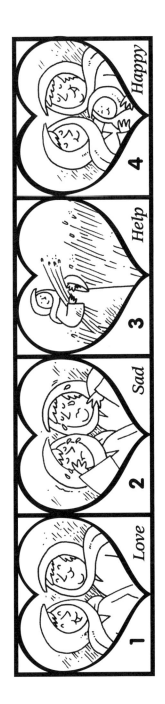

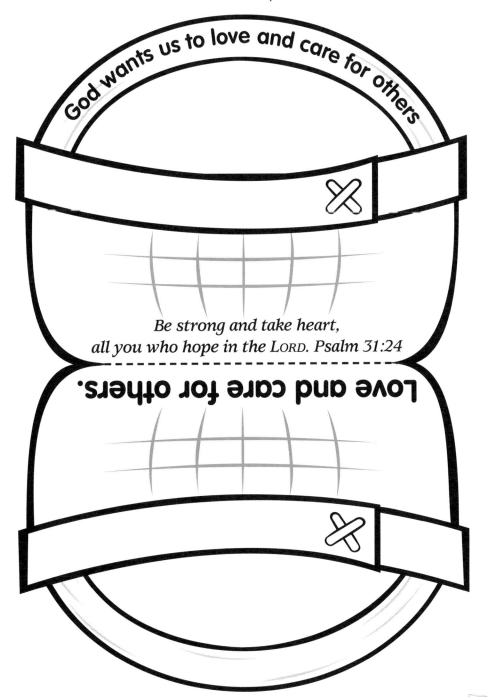

God wants us to love and care for others

Be strong and take heart, all you who hope in the LORD. Psalm 31:24

Love and care for others.

Splash-n-Spray

Use these *Splash-n-Spray* activities to build knowledge that enriches the children's experience with the lesson while having fun.

Get List:
- Index cards
- Scissors
- Marker
- Basket

Bible Story Link

Gathering Grain

Cut the index cards into two-inch long ovals as if each is a piece of grain. Make two or more pieces per child. Put a small mark on three or four pieces of grain and place all the grain in a basket. Gather the children and tell them they'll learn about a woman in the Bible who gathered grain to show love and care for another woman. Scatter the grain. Have each child gather two pieces. Let the children who have the marked pieces tell about a time when they were kind to someone or when someone showed kindness to them. Collect the grain in the basket and play again until all have had a chance to share.

Get List:
- None

Game

Naomi, Naomi, Ruth!

Have the children sit in a circle to play this variation of Duck, Duck, Goose. Explain that instead of saying, "duck" we will say, "Naomi" and instead of saying, "goose" we will say, "Ruth." Tell the children that just as "Ruth" will get up and run after whoever tagged them, Ruth in the Bible got up and went with her mother-in-law Naomi to show love for her. Let each child returning to the circle after the chase catch some breath and then tell one way we can show love for others.

Get List:
- Different colored rolls of streamers

Extension Activity

Ribbons of Love

Cut a three-foot streamer for each child. **Today's Bible story teaches us to love and care for others. Our game shows how putting our love together can make a big difference.** Have all the children stand together and choose a partner. Give each child a streamer to use with their partner's to make a heart on the floor. Have everyone pick up their streamers and regroup in threes to make larger hearts on the floor. Continue regrouping in larger numbers making increasingly larger hearts until you make one big heart.

Soak It In
Bible Story Hands-on Activities

These activities can be used with large or small groups or as individual stations.

Get List:
- Small tortillas
- Paper plates
- Jelly
- Craft sticks
- Napkins

Activity 1

Spreading Love

Give each child a tortilla on a paper plate. Explain that the bread the women in the Bible story made was a type of flatbread, similar to a tortilla, but not as thin. Nevertheless, the women shared bread to spread love to others. Have children use craft sticks to spread some jelly, like love, over their tortillas. Enjoy and talk about ways to spread love to others. *Note: Check with parents for food allergies.*

Get List:
- 4 baskets
- 4 or more beanbags
- 4 pieces of paper
- Masking tape
- Marker

Activity 2

Basket Toss

Be strong and take heart, all you who hope in the LORD. (Psalm 31:24)

Put a line of tape on the floor. Place the baskets about five feet from the line. Put a piece of paper in front of each basket that has a part of the Bible Verse written on it. Players stand behind the line and toss beanbags into the baskets. At each basket, they shout out the part of the Bible Verse that is in front of that basket.

Get List:
- Cardstock
- Scissors
- Marker
- Whole grain cereal
- Glue

Activity 3

Stick It to Others

Cut a heart from the cardstock for each child. Write this lesson's Bible Truth, "God wants us to love and care for others," on each heart. Have the children spread glue over the heart or in a design then sprinkle whole grain cereal on the glue. Press down gently on the cereal to help it stick. Talk about how the grain stuck on the heart can remind us of how Ruth stayed with Naomi out of love. Talk with the children about ways we can show love to others, making our love stick with them.

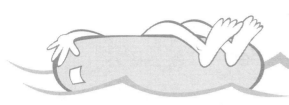

Soak It In
Bible Story Time

Get List:
- Bible
- Completed *Flippers Up* baskets made from the reproducible on page 25
- Story strip pictures from the reproducible page

Have your stacks of story strip pictures from the *Flippers Up* construction ready to use as indicated in the Bible story. Gather the children for story time. Be sure they have their *Flippers Up* baskets with them. Open your Bible to the book of Ruth and show the children where this story if located.

The book of Ruth is an amazing story of two women, Ruth and Naomi, and how they showed love to each other. Earlier you colored story pictures that we will use in this story. You have your baskets to hold the story pictures you collect. Scatter all the pictures numbered 1. Tell the children to pick up a card, but not the one they colored. Explain you want them to have a card someone else colored, and it doesn't matter who. **This first story picture shows Ruth and Naomi. Ruth is the young one and Naomi is older.**

The word *Love* is on the picture because Naomi and Ruth loved each other and God. Ruth was married to Naomi's son. Everyone was happy and life was good. But then something very sad happened.

Scatter picture 2. Have the children get a picture and look at it. **Naomi's husband died and Ruth's husband died. Ruth and Naomi were very sad because they missed their husbands and they had no money since their husbands died. That's why your picture has the word *Sad* on it. But Ruth and Naomi still loved each other and cared for each other because they both knew that was what God wanted them to do.** Put picture 2 in the baskets.

Scatter picture 3. Have the children get one each and look at it. **This picture says *Help* because Ruth is helping to gather grain for herself and Naomi. She would have put the grain in a basket. Gathering grain was hard work. Ruth wanted to do that work to be helpful and show love and care for Naomi. Ruth and Naomi ground the grain into flour that they used to bake bread. Now they had food to eat.** Put picture 3 away.

Scatter picture 4. Have the children get one each and look at it. **This last picture says *Happy* because something very happy happened. While Ruth was gathering grain in the field, she met a man named Boaz. Boaz loved and cared for Ruth. Soon, Ruth and Boaz got married and later had a son named Obed. Naomi, Ruth and Boaz loved Obed and cared for him. Our picture shows Naomi and Ruth with Obed.** Tell the children to put picture 4 in their baskets with the other story pictures.

God wants us to love and care for each other just as Naomi, Ruth and Boaz loved and cared for each other. When we love and care for others we will have happy hearts too.

- **Who loved and cared for Naomi?** *(Ruth)*
- **Why did Naomi and Ruth love and care for each other?** *(they knew that was what God wanted them to do)*
- **Who should we love and care for?** *(others)*

Sail Away

Get List:
- Basket
- Paper
- Scissors
- Marker

Prayer

Cut a small paper heart for each child and collect the hearts in a basket. Have the children sit in a circle. Pass the basket for each child to take a heart. Ask each of the children, one at a time, to name someone they will show love and care for. Write that name on one side and the child's name on the other to make a Prayer Heart. Pass the basket to collect the hearts. Then lead the children in this prayer: **Dear God, thank you for all the people whose names are on our hearts. Help us to love and care for others. In Jesus' name, amen.**

Get List:
- Large baskets

Cleanup

Provide some baskets for the children. Have them pretend they are picking up grain as they clean up, filling the baskets with things to put away or throw away. As they put things into the basket have them say, "Fill our baskets full of joy when we care for girls and boys."

Get List:
- Completed *Flippers Up*
- Basketful of hearts with names on them
- Copy of *Home Connection* for each child

Homeward Bound

As the children leave, make sure they have the completed *Flippers Up* they made for Bible Story Time and the *Home Connection* from page 30. Return each child's Prayer Heart from your Prayer Time. Tell them their heart can remind them to show the love and care God wants us to show others.

- What will you do to show this person you love and care for him or her?
- Who wants us to show love and care for others?

PINT-SIZE BIBLE BITES

Obed, the baby in this story, was also born in Bethlehem like Jesus. He eventually becomes the grandfather to King David.

TEACHER TIP

If children are having a hard time sitting and listening to the Bible story, be sure they know what is expected of them during this time. You might designate a special story spot marked with an "x" or put down small carpet squares. These designate an area that helps young children idenfify boundaries and provide some helpful structure.

Home Connection
Dive In!

Title: Great Love (Valentine's Day)

Bible Story: Ruth 1—4

Bible Truth: God wants us to love and care for others.

Bible Verse: Be strong and take heart, all you who hope in the LORD. (Psalm 31:24)

- In this lesson your child **heard** the Bible story of how Ruth loved and cared for Naomi.

- In this lesson your child **learned** that the love and care we show others can make them happy.

- In this lesson your child **remembered** that God wants us to show love and care to others.

This Bible story is about a young woman named Ruth and her mother-in-law, Naomi, who both became widows. Both Ruth and Naomi suffered for they had no husbands or any means to find food or make money. They struggled in many ways but always had plenty of love and care for each other. God honored all their hard work and turned their sorrow into joy. Teach your little one that planting kindness and showing love and care toward others will produce a harvest of great joy.

HOME CONNECTIONS

These are items used during the Bible story lesson that might be commonly found in your home. When your child sees or plays with one of the items mentioned below, help make the connection to the Bible story.

Hearts: Hearts were used throughout the lesson as a reminder to love and care for others. Every time you see a heart, remind your child of the great love God has for us and that he wants us to share that love with others.

Baskets: In the lesson children filled baskets and tossed beanbags into baskets. They serve as reminders of the baskets used to gather grain in the Bible story. When you use a basket, remind your child of how Ruth showed great love and care toward Naomi by gathering grain in her basket.

KEEPING CONNECTED

Here are two simple activities that were used in class during the Bible story lesson, Great Love. Use these activities to help your child remember the Bible story lesson.

Ribbons of Love

Cut different lengths of streamers. Help your child lay them out on the floor to make heart shapes of different sizes. Talk about how our actions, whether big or small, show the love in our hearts for others. Talk about people who love and care for your child. Then talk about ways your child can show love and care toward others.

Basket Toss

Place a basket on the floor about five feet away from your child. Provide an item for your child to toss into the basket. When your child hits the basket, you can shout out the Bible Verse listed at the top of the page.

Prayer

Just before tucking your child into bed, use a washable marker to draw a small heart on the back of your child's hand, saying this is a reminder that Jesus loves and cares for us. Then say how much you love and care for your child too! Say this prayer together: **Dear God, thank you for your love for me. Thank you for the people who love and care for me. Help me to love and care for others. In Jesus' name, amen.**

Lesson 4

JESUS PRAYED FOR YOU

(NATIONAL DAY OF PRAYER)

Bible Story: John 17

Bible Truth: Jesus loves you and prayed for you.

Bible Verse: "Do not let your hearts be troubled. Trust in God; trust also in me." (John 14:1)

A foundational need in the lives of children everywhere is to know they are loved and to be able to trust someone. Introduce the children to the person who is the only one who can ultimately fill this need—Jesus. In this Bible story the children learn that Jesus loves and cares for them. In fact, the Creator of the universe prayed for each and every one of them.

- In this lesson children will **hear** the Bible story of when Jesus prayed for himself, for his disciples and for all believers.

- In this lesson children will **learn** that they are so important to Jesus that he prayed for each of them.

- In this lesson children will **remember** they can trust Jesus because he loves, cares and prays for them.

LESSON FOUR SNAPSHOT

Flippers Up
Reproducible Page

- [ ] 1 copy of the *Flippers Up* reproducible on page 33 for each child
- [ ] Scissors
- [ ] Crayons or markers
- [ ] Tape

Splash-n-Spray

Bible Story Link:
A Talk with God
- [ ] Bible or Bible storybook
- [ ] CD player
- [ ] Music CD

Game:
Morning, Noon or Night
- [ ] 2 pieces of paper
- [ ] Markers
- [ ] Tape

Extension Activity:
Prayer Song
- [ ] None

Soak It In
Bible Story
Hands-on Activities

Activity 1:
PRAY
- [ ] Paper plates
- [ ] Markers
- [ ] Spoons
- [ ] Pretzel sticks
- [ ] Raisins
- [ ] Apple slices
- [ ] Yogurt

Activity 2:
Praying for You
- [ ] 4 index cards
- [ ] 4 bowls
- [ ] Marker

Activity 3:
Following Jesus
- [ ] Construction paper
- [ ] Scissors

Bible Story Time
- [ ] Bible
- [ ] Completed *Flippers Up* made from the reproducible page

Sail Away

Prayer
- [ ] None

Cleanup
- [ ] None

Homeward Bound
- [ ] Completed *Flippers Up*
- [ ] Copy of *Home Connection* from page 38 for each child

HEART OF THE STORY

How amazing is it to think that Jesus prayed for you? In John 17 Jesus prays for himself, for the disciples and for all future believers. That means he prayed for you. He prayed for unity, protection and holiness for all followers of Christ. Teach your little ones to trust Jesus because he loves and prays for each and every one of them. As you teach the children, take comfort and confidence in the fact that Jesus prayed for you to help you touch the lives of these children and to further his kingdom.

Flippers Up
Bible Story Reproducible Page

Get List:
- A copy of the reproducible on this page for each child
- Scissors
- Crayons or marker
- Tape

Copy and cut out the reproducible. Have the children color pictures 1 and 2, then draw themselves in 3. Cut on line A to separate the picture strip. Cut out the two narrow rectangles as indicated. Roll the large piece from the narrow end, aligning the slits to insert the picture strip. Tape the edge as indicated. Show the children how the story strip slides through their telescope.

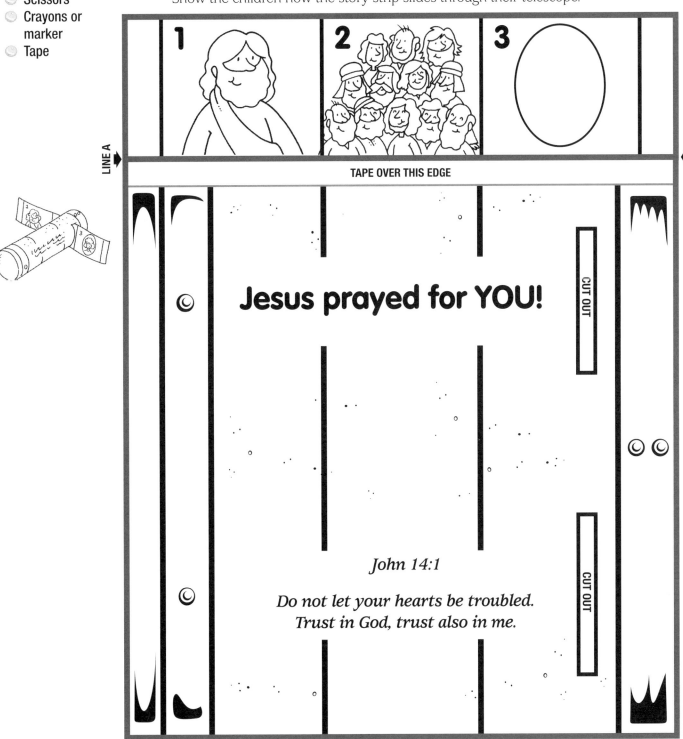

LINE A

LINE A

TAPE OVER THIS EDGE

Jesus prayed for YOU!

CUT OUT

CUT OUT

John 14:1

Do not let your hearts be troubled.
Trust in God, trust also in me.

Splash-n-Spray

Use these *Splash-n-Spray* activities to build knowledge that enriches the children's experience with the lesson while having fun.

Get List:
- Bible or Bible storybook
- CD player
- Music CD

Bible Story Link

Doing What Jesus Asked

Have the children sit in a circle with you. Explain that Jesus prayed for us, asking his Father to help us be good friends and to help us know Jesus. Explore how God is already doing this. Start the music and pass your Bible or storybook (since both help us know Jesus) to your friend on your right. Stop the music and ask the child holding the book to tell something he or she already knows about Jesus. Continue around the circle, passing the book carefully and sharing what we know about Jesus.

Get List:
- 2 pieces of paper
- Markers
- Tape

Game

Morning, Noon or Night

Write "morning" and draw a sunrise on a paper that you tape to a wall at one end of your classroom. At the opposite end tape a picture of the sun at noon and write "noon" on it. Call out, **We can pray in the** _____ (fill in the blank with morning, noon or night). The children run to the appropriate sign, but when you say night, they run to the center of the room and lay down on the floor.

Get List:
- None

Extension Activity

Prayer Song

Lead the children in the following prayer, or sing it to the tune of the *Doxology* with the following motions:

Come, Lord, and hear our grateful praise.
(motion as if you are beckoning someone towards you)
We can talk with you on all our days.
(push hands outwards with palms up in a giving motion)
Help us to give our best to you,
(lift hands upwards, toward God)
And to your Word
(position hands as if a book)
we will be true.
(hands over heart)

Soak It In
Bible Story Hands-on Activities

These activities can be used with large or small groups or as individual stations.

Get List:
- Paper plates
- Markers
- Spoons
- Pretzel sticks
- Raisins
- Apple slices
- Yogurt

PRAY

Have each child print *pray* in large letters on a plate. Then have them place food items under the correct letter: P—Pretzels, R—Raisins, A—Apples and Y—Yogurt. Talk about how the name of each food begins with a letter in the word *pray*. Explain how the plate reminds us that Jesus prayed for us and that we can pray for others. *Note: Check with parents for food allergies.*

Get List:
- 4 index cards
- 4 bowls
- Marker

Praying for You

"Do not let your hearts be troubled. Trust in God; trust also in me." (John 14:1)

On each of the four index cards write a part of the Bible Verse. Spread the cards on the table, and turn a bowl upside down over each card as a protective covering. **Jesus prayed for you and for your protection.** Have the children move the bowls around, keeping the cards protected under each bowl. Then lift the bowls and have the children say the Bible Verse aloud. **Were the bowls in the correct order?** Cover the cards and move them again to get the Bible Verse in the correct order.

Get List:
- Construction paper
- Scissors

Following Jesus

Cut out three paper footprints for each child. Explain that Jesus prayed for everyone who follows him by loving God and other people as he did. That is sort of like following in his footsteps, walking behind him. Pretend the footprints are Jesus' footprints. Have the children walk in Jesus' footprints, putting two down to stand on while placing the third a step away. Take a step to the third footprint. Then lean back to retrieve the first one, moving it forward to take another step. Have the children walk this way, in Jesus' footprints, from one end of the room to the other. Let them race. As they go, have them repeat, "We're following Jesus you can see, we're following Jesus, he prayed for me."

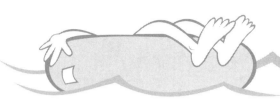

Soak It In
Bible Story Time

Get List:
- Bible
- Completed *Flippers Up* made from the reproducible page

Gather the children for story time. Be sure they have their *Flippers Up* ready to go. Hold up a Bible for the children to see. **In the Bible in the book of John we learn there is someone who prayed for us because he loves us. Do you know who that is?** Let the children respond. **Jesus prayed for us. As he prayed, Jesus looked up toward heaven.**

Show me your telescopes. We use telescopes to look toward the heavens and the stars. Jesus looked toward heaven, and he began to pray. Jesus prayed for three things. When I say, <u>one, two, three,</u> I want you to shout "Jesus prayed for me!" then look into your telescopes. Let's practice. <u>One, two, three</u>! *(children say, Jesus prayed for me! and look into their telescopes)* During our Bible story, you'll look into your telescopes to see who Jesus prayed for.

Slide picture 1 into your telescope and look. Who do you see? *(Jesus)* Yes, it is a picture of Jesus and a clue to who Jesus prayed for first—himself. The Bible tells us Jesus talked with God, his Father, about things he was thinking about and events he wanted to happen. We can also tell God what we think about and what we want to see happen.

But that's not all Jesus prayed for. Slide picture 2 into your telescope. <u>One, two, three</u>! *(children say, Jesus prayed for me! and look into their telescopes)* Who do you see? *(people, men, 12 men)* This shows the 12 men who followed Jesus. They were called disciples. Jesus loved his disciples and prayed for them too. Jesus asked God to keep them safe, help them be friends and to help them live the way Jesus taught them.

Jesus wasn't finished praying. He prayed for more people. Let's find out who. Move picture 3 into your telescopes. <u>One, two, three</u>! *(children say, Jesus prayed for me! and look into their telescopes)* Who do you see? *(me)* That's right! Jesus prayed for you. Jesus prayed for each one of us because he loves every one of us. We are important to him. He prayed that we would be good friends who help each other know Jesus and do what he wants. That's what we're doing right now!

- Who prayed for you? *(Jesus)*
- Why did Jesus pray for you? *(because he loves me and cares for me)*

Sail Away

Get List:
- None

Prayer

Have everyone put up one finger and tell who Jesus prayed for first. Then have them raise two fingers and tell who Jesus prayed for second. Tell everyone to put up three fingers and say, **one, two, three.** Let the children respond as they did in the story. Explain that we can pray for others too. Ask the children who they would like to pray for. Lead them in this prayer: **Dear God, thank you for loving and caring for us. Thank you for our friends. Please help our friends and protect them. In Jesus' name, amen.**

Get List:
- None

Cleanup

When Jesus prayed he looked toward heaven. When some people pray they pray on their knees. Have the children pick up toys while they are on their knees. Then remind them that praying is talking to God and telling him what you are thinking, feeling, wondering about or what concerns you.

Get List:
- Completed *Flippers Up*
- Copy of *Home Connection* for each child

Homeward Bound

As the children leave, make sure they have their completed *Flippers Up* they made for Bible Story Time and the *Home Connection* from page 38. As they leave, say to each one, **one, two, three** and let them respond. Give 'em a high five or a hug as appropriate.

- Who prayed for you because he loves you?
- Tell me one thing you will remember when you look to heaven.

PINT-SIZE BIBLE BITES

Jesus' prayer in John 17 is the longest recorded prayer of Jesus that we have.

TEACHER TIP

Many times children think praying is something we do when we close our eyes, fold our hands and repeat what someone is saying. Begin to teach your little ones how prayer is chatting with God anytime, anywhere, with eyes closed or eyes open if necessary. Little children are very open to this idea.

Home Connection
Dive In!

Title: Jesus Prayed for You
(National Day of Prayer)

Bible Story: John 17

Bible Truth: Jesus loves you and prayed for you.

Bible Verse: "Do not let your hearts be troubled. Trust in God; trust also in me." (John 14:1)

- In this lesson your child **heard** the Bible story of when Jesus prayed for himself, for the disciples and for all believers.

- In this lesson your child **learned** that he or she is so important to Jesus that he prayed for him or her.

- In this lesson your child **remembered** to trust Jesus because he loves, cares and prays for him or her.

In this Bible passage your child learned that Jesus prayed. Jesus prayed for himself, telling God, his Father, what was on his heart. Your child can tell God what is on his or her heart too. Then Jesus prayed for his 12 disciples. Your child can follow Jesus too. Finally, your child learned that Jesus prayed for all believers. Show your child he or she can trust Jesus, because he loves your child.

HOME CONNECTIONS

These are items used during the Bible story lesson that might be commonly found in your home. When your child sees or plays with the item mentioned below, help make the connection to the Bible story.

The numbers 1, 2, 3: These numbers were used throughout the Bible story and the lesson activities. Anytime you hear or see these numbers, remind your child that, "1, 2, 3: Jesus prays for you and me!"

Looking up: The *Flippers Up* that has come home is a telescope. The telescope reminds us that Jesus looked up to the heavens when he prayed. Review the Bible story with your child as you look at the pictures of the three things Jesus prayed for: himself, his disciples and you!

KEEPING CONNECTED

Here are two simple activities that were used in class during the Bible story lesson, Jesus Prayed for

You. Use these activities to help your child remember the Bible story lesson.

Following Jesus

Cut out three large footprints from paper or paper bags. Have your child walk across the room by placing the footprints on the floor, stepping on two of them, reaching back to pick up the third and then moving it forward to be stepped on. As your child moves across the floor, have your child repeat, **"I'm following Jesus you can see, I'm following Jesus he prayed for me!"**

Flippers Up

The *Flippers Up* that has come home is a telescope. The telescope was used because when Jesus prayed, he looked up to the heavens. Review the Bible story with your child as you look at the pictures. The pictures will remind your child of the three things Jesus prayed for: himself, his disciples and you!

Prayer

It is extremely powerful to know that someone is praying for you. Share a bedtime prayer tonight that lets your child know you are praying directly for him or her. Say this prayer: **Dear God, thank you for _____ (name of child) and the blessing he/she is to our family. Protect him/her and help him/her through each day. May _____ know that Jesus loves him/her. In Jesus' name, amen.**

Lesson 5

COURTLY COURAGE

Bible Story: Esther 2—8

Bible Truth: Trust God. He is in control.

Bible Verse: Have I not commanded you? Be strong and courageous. (Joshua 1:9)

In a world that seems pretty out of control, young children need to know God is ultimately in control. No matter how grim the situation looks, your little ones need to know they can trust God. As you teach the story of Queen Esther, let the children know that they, too, can be courageous and strong, because with God all things are possible.

- In this lesson children will **hear** the Bible story of how God protected his people through Queen Esther.

- In this lesson children will **learn** that God is in control when things might seem out of control.

- In this lesson children will **remember** to trust God because he is in control.

LESSON FIVE SNAPSHOT

Flippers Up
Reproducible Page

- [ ] Copies of page 41 for each child
- [ ] Scissors
- [ ] Paper plate (one per child)
- [ ] Crayons or markers
- [ ] Metal brad
- [ ] Pen or pencil
- [ ] Aluminum foil
- [ ] Glue

Splash-n-Spray

Bible Story Link:
God's People
- [ ] Pennies
- [ ] Quarters (more quarters than pennies)
- [ ] Special treat (candy, marshmallows, etc.)

Game:
King and Queen
- [ ] Aluminum foil

Extension Activity:
"Xerxes Says"
Balancing Game
- [ ] None

Soak It In
Bible Story Hands-on Activities

Activity 1:
A Royal Treat
- [ ] Paper plates
- [ ] Cotton swab
- [ ] Food coloring
- [ ] Bowls for food coloring
- [ ] Assorted fresh fruit chunks

Activity 2:
Be Strong
- [ ] Construction paper
- [ ] Tape
- [ ] Inflated balloons (two per child)
- [ ] Markers

Activity 3:
At the Palace
- [ ] Building materials such as blocks

Bible Story Time
- [ ] Bible
- [ ] Completed *Flippers Up* made from the reproducible page

Sail Away

Prayer
- [ ] Pretend scepter (drumstick, paper towel tube, etc.)

Cleanup
- [ ] Pretend scepter

Homeward Bound
- [ ] Completed *Flippers Up*
- [ ] Copy of *Home Connection* from page 46 for each child

HEART OF THE STORY

Have you ever felt your heart sink to your toes, wondering why something terrible has happened to you? Then you have felt the same thing Queen Esther felt. If she tried to talk to the king without permission, she would surely be put to death. But if she did nothing, the king's new decree would put all the Jews to death. In this Bible story we see there was no natural way out of this awful situation. But through God, who was ultimately in control, the story has a happy ending. Some of your children today may have lives that seem out of control. Empower them with God's love. Let them know that just like in this Bible story, God is in control.

Flippers Up
Bible Story Reproducible Page

Get List:
- A copy of the reproducible on this page for each child
- Scissors
- Paper plate (one per child)
- Crayons or markers
- Metal brads
- Pen or pencil
- Aluminum foil
- Glue

Color the pictures. Have the children glue on small pieces of foil for crowns or jewels. Cut out the large circle and make a hole in the center. Cut out a quarter section of each paper plate. Put a hole in the center of the plates. Place the circle behind the paper plate. Push the metal brad through the center holes to attach the two items. Turn the paper plate to reveal each picture.

Queen Esther

Curtsy

King X

Bow Down

Haman the Horrible

Shake Hands

Mordecai

God's Man

Splash-n-Spray

Use these *Splash-n-Spray* activities to build knowledge that enriches the children's experience with the lesson while having fun.

Get List:
- Pennies
- Quarters (more quarters than pennies)
- Special treat (candy, marshmallows, etc.)

God's People

You'll need enough coins for every child. Explain that quarters will represent Jews, or God's chosen people, and pennies will represent all other people. Have the children sit in a circle with their hands cupped together in their laps. Secretly place in their hands either a penny or a quarter. When finished, have the children with the quarters stand. Remind them they are Jews, God's chosen people. Explain how God loved his people, but they were not always treated well. Give them a special treat, and tell them they'll learn more about the Jews in the Bible story. Gather the coins, and play again until everyone has had a chance to be Jewish!

Get List:
- Aluminum foil

King and Queen

Have the children sit in a circle. Using the foil, make two crowns. Choose a player to be king/queen, placing a crown on that child's head. Give the other crown to the same child. That child takes the crown and walks around the circle, behind the other children. The king /queen asks, "Will you be … " and pretends to place the crown on everyone's head. The king/queen eventually picks someone and asks, "Will you be … my queen/king ?" The king/queen places the crown on the chosen child's head. The king/queen runs around the circle, chased by the chosen child. If the chosen child tags the king/queen before he or she returns to sit in his or her original spot, then the chasing child becomes the new king or queen. Otherwise, the original king remains king for another turn.

Get List:
- None

"Xerxes Says" Balancing Game

This game is similar to Simon Says. The first difference is that "Xerxes" always has to "say" because it is not about trickery, but balance and control. The other difference is that everyone begins by standing on one leg. Give the children a minute to see if they can balance. Then give them different instructions (touch your nose; wiggle your fingers; clap your hands; pretend to sneeze; say, "Jesus loves you"). When a child cannot follow the instruction while remaining on one foot, they are out (or if you don't want to play with outs, let everyone continue playing and laughing at the challenge of the game). When the game is over say, **"It was hard to control our bodies and stay balanced in that game. But we know that God has control over everything. We can listen to the God who is in control."**

Soak It In
Bible Story Hands-on Activities

These activities can be used with large or small groups or as individual stations.

Get List:
- Paper plates
- Cotton swab
- Food coloring
- Bowls for food coloring
- Assorted fresh fruit chunks

A Royal Treat

On each paper plate draw a crown using a cotton swab dipped in food coloring. Have the children fill their crowns with fruit jewels. Discuss how kings and queens wear crowns. **Kings and queens are important people who rule over the people of their land. In our Bible story today, we'll learn about a very special queen named Esther.** *Note: Check with parents for food allergies.*

Get List:
- Construction paper
- Tape
- Inflated balloons (two per child)
- Markers

Be Strong

Have I not commanded you? Be strong and courageous. (Joshua 1:9)

On the construction paper, have the children write the Bible Verse. The children will use the items to make a dumbbell. Have them roll the paper and tape it to make the dumbbell bar. Attach balloons on each end of the paper roll. The children can "work out" as they say the Bible Verse together. Discuss how they'll learn that Queen Esther had to be strong and courageous.

Get List:
- Building materials such as blocks

At the Palace

Kings and queens, especially in biblical times, lived in large, beautiful palaces. Let's use our building materials to build a large palace. Today we're going to learn about Queen Esther, who lived in a large palace.

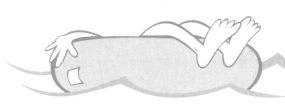

Soak It In
Bible Story Time

Get List:
- Bible
- Completed *Flippers Up* made from the reproducible page

Gather the children for story time. Be sure they have their *Flippers Up* ready to go. Let me introduce you to some people in today's Bible story. Whenever you see me curtsy, like this (demonstrate), you curtsy too, and turn to Queen Esther's picture. If you see me bow down, turn to King Xerxes' or King X's picture. Turn to Mordecai's picture. We will turn to this picture of Mordecai when I point to heaven with both pointer fingers and flex my muscles. Mordecai is a Jew, one of God's chosen people. When I shake my fist and boo, turn to Haman's picture. We'll call him Haman the Horrible. He was mean especially to the Jews.

Hold up a Bible for the children to see. There is a book in the Bible called Esther. Today we'll learn how Queen Esther trusted God to save her people, the Jews. Esther (curtsy) was a beautiful, young Jewish woman. The king (bow) loved her very much. There was a wicked man (shake fist angrily), Haman, who worked for King Xerxes (bow). Haman (shake fist) did not like the Jews. Haman (shake fist) was up to no good and tricked King Xerxes (bow) into making a law that would kill all the Jews. The law made Queen Esther's (curtsy) heart very sad. Queen Esther (curtsy) had a cousin named Mordecai (point). He was a Jew and a man who loved God very much. Mordecai (point) told Queen Esther (curtsy) how scared all the Jews were that they were going to die. What was Queen Esther (curtsy) going to do? Could she save her people, the Jews?

If Queen Esther (curtsy) went to talk to King Xerxes (bow) without his permission, she would surely be put to death. Queen Esther (curtsy) was scared, but she knew God wanted her to do the right thing, so she went to talk to King Xerxes (bow). Queen Esther (curtsy) asked Mordecai (point) and all the Jews to pray for her while she went to talk to the king.

When Queen Esther (curtsy) went to King Xerxes (bow), Haman (shake fists) was there too. Queen Esther (curtsy) asked King Xerxes (bow) not to kill her and the Jews. The king (bow) had no idea what Queen Esther (curtsy) was talking about because he had been tricked by Haman (shake fist). Once King Xerxes (bow) knew what was going on, he stopped that mean man, Haman (shake fist). He kicked Haman (shake fist) out and put Mordecai (point) in his place.

The Jews were saved, and everyone was happy. God used Queen Esther (curtsy) to save his people. Queen Esther (curtsy) took a big chance in saving her people, the Jews. She knew God was in control. Queen Esther (curtsy) knew God would help her find a way to save the Jews, and he did.

- Even when things did not seem to be going well, who was in control? *(God)*
- How did Queen Esther help the Jews? *(by being brave and talking to King Xerxes)*
- Who did Queen Esther trust to help her? *(God)*

Sail Away

Get List:
- Pretend scepter (drumstick, paper towel tube, etc.)

Prayer

Pass the "royal" scepter from child to child. As the children pass the scepter, have them tell you one thing they remember from the Bible story. Then lead them in this prayer: **Dear God, thank you for always being in control. Help us to trust you, especially when things get tough. Help us to remember you are always with us. In Jesus' name, amen.**

Get List:
- Pretend scepter

Cleanup

As the children are cleaning up, walk around the room with the royal scepter. Before the children can pick up or put an item away, they must bow and say, "God is in control."

Get List:
- Completed *Flippers Up*
- Copy of *Home Connection* for each child

Homeward Bound

As the children leave, make sure they have their completed *Flippers Up* they made for Bible Story Time. As the children leave, tell them their *Flippers Up* reminds you of all the people in the Bible story.

- Who was the person who was strong and courageous in our story?
- Who's always in control in our lives no matter what?

PINT-SIZE BIBLE BITES

Before Esther became queen, she had a different name. Hadassah was her Jewish name. After she became queen, her name was changed to a Babylonian one—Esther.

TEACHER TIP

Jews, kings and queens are not common concepts with children, except for movies, stories or cartoons they may have seen with such characters. Take time to explain and clarify these concepts that were prevalent during biblical times.

Home Connection
Dive In!

Title: Courtly Courage

Bible Story: Esther 2—8

Bible Truth: Trust God. He is in control.

Bible Verse: Have I not commanded you? Be strong and courageous. (Joshua 1:9)

- In this lesson your child **heard** the Bible story of how God protected his people through Queen Esther.

- In this lesson your child **learned** that God is in control when things might seem out of control.

- In this lesson your child **remembered** to trust God because he is in control.

In this Bible story, a king is tricked into making a law that will end up terminating the lives of all the Jews. Queen Esther goes before the king to plead for their lives, including her own. It took an incredible amount of courage on Esther's behalf to take a stand for the Jews; in fact, she was certain she was going to die. From Esther's story we can learn that even when things seem out of control, God is ultimately in control. We just need to trust him. Teach your little ones to trust in the one and only sure thing—God!

HOME CONNECTIONS

These are items used during the Bible story lesson that might be commonly found in your home. When your child sees or plays with one of the items mentioned below, help make the connection to the Bible story.

Foil: Foil was used in the lesson to make crowns. The next time you use foil, make a little crown. Talk about kings and queens you know from movies, books or Bible stories.

Blocks: We used blocks to teach about palaces. The children learned that kings and queens, especially in biblical times, lived in large, beautiful palaces. Provide blocks for your child to build a palace.

KEEPING CONNECTED

Here are two simple activities that were used in class during the Bible story lesson, Courtly Courage. Use these activities to help your child remember the Bible story lesson.

Be Strong

On construction paper, help your child write the Bible Verse (see above). Your child will use this to make a dumbbell. Have your child roll the piece of paper and tape it to make the bar. Then attach balloons on each end of the paper roll. Your child can "work out" while saying the Bible Verse. Discuss how we can be strong and courageous like Queen Esther.

A Royal Treat

On a paper plate draw a crown using a cotton swab dipped in food coloring. Have your child decorate the crown with fresh fruit pieces for jewels. Explain how kings and queens are important people who wear crowns and rule over the people of their land.

Prayer

After you kiss your little prince or princess good night, say this prayer: **Dear God, thank you for _____ (fill in name). May he/she be filled with courage. May he/she learn to trust you and know that you, God, are always in control. In Jesus' name, amen.**

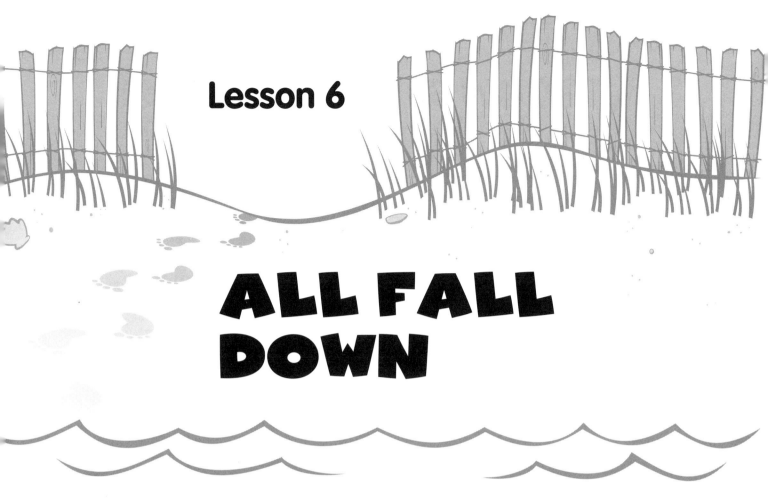

Lesson 6

ALL FALL DOWN

Bible Story: Joshua 6:1–20

Bible Truth: God is powerful. His way is the right way.

Bible Verse: But thanks be to God! He gives us the victory through our Lord Jesus Christ. (1 Corinthians 15:57)

Marching, shouting, tooting horns, rumbling and finally, tumbling, the walls come crashing down. This lesson is packed with action. Be sure the children focus on God as the one who made those walls come down. God is powerful, and his way is always the right way to do things.

- In this lesson children will **hear** the story of how God used Joshua to bring down the walls of the city of Jericho.

- In this lesson children will **learn** that God loves and cares for his people.

- In this lesson children will **remember** God is powerful and his way is the right way to do things.

LESSON SIX SNAPSHOT

Flippers Up
Reproducible Page

- ☐ Copies of page 49 for each child
- ☐ Crayons or markers
- ☐ Tape
- ☐ Scissors

Splash-n-Spray

Bible Story Link:
God's People
- ☐ None

Game:
All Fall Down
- ☐ None

Extension Activity:
Picturing God's Power
- ☐ Crayons or washable markers
- ☐ Butcher paper or construction paper
- ☐ Optional: Scissors and glue

Soak It In
Bible Story
Hands-on Activities

Activity 1:
Walls of Jericho
- ☐ Paper plates
- ☐ Large marshmallows
- ☐ Graham crackers divided into fourths

Activity 2:
God's Winners
- ☐ Construction paper
- ☐ Tape
- ☐ Scissors
- ☐ Streamers
- ☐ Markers

Activity 3:
Wall of Jericho
- ☐ Building blocks

Bible Story Time
- ☐ Bible
- ☐ Completed *Flippers Up* made from the reproducible page

Sail Away

Prayer
- ☐ None

Cleanup
- ☐ None

Homeward Bound
- ☐ Completed *Flippers Up*
- ☐ Copy of *Home Connection* from page 54 for each child

HEART OF THE STORY

Have you ever felt like God's plans for you weren't exactly what you were expecting? Or have you ever had to face what seemed like insurmountable odds? Joshua and the Israelites were taken from their homeland and kept in slavery. God was now restoring them back to their homeland. They stood before the huge city walls of Jericho in disbelief. Joshua told them that God's plan to take the city was to march around the wall for seven days and then shout. What kind of battle plan was that? Joshua never doubted God, nor should we. Teach the children that God is powerful. He can do anything. He will do amazing things if we follow him.

Flippers Up
Bible Story Reproducible Page

Get List:
- A copy of the reproducible on this page for each child
- Crayons or markers
- Tape
- Scissors

Color and cut out the horn. Fold and tape it together where indicated. Bend it in slightly as you hold the trumpet to round out the shape.

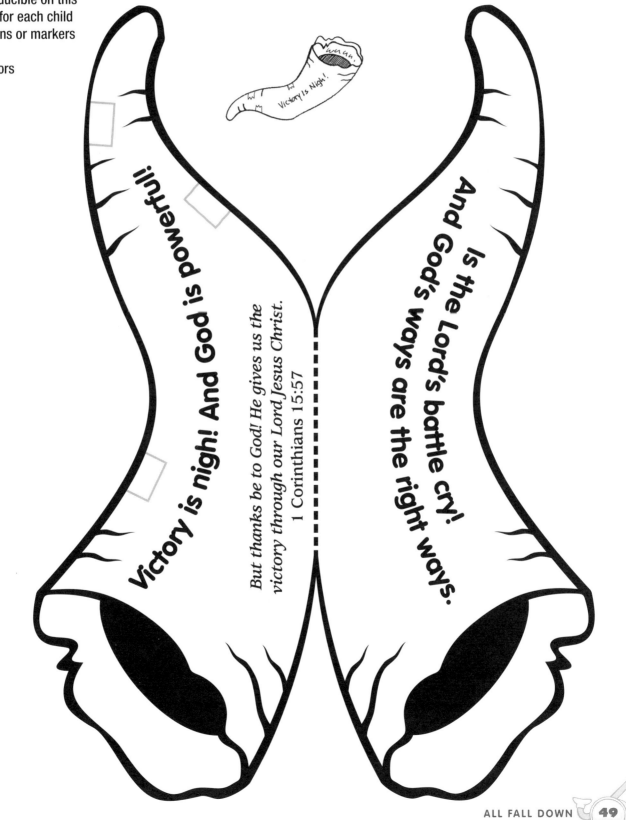

Victory is nigh! And God is powerful!

But thanks be to God! He gives us the victory through our Lord Jesus Christ. 1 Corinthians 15:57

Is the Lord's battle cry! And God's ways are the right ways.

Splash-n-Spray

Use these *Splash-n-Spray* activities to build knowledge that enriches the children's experience with the lesson while having fun.

Get List:
- None

Bible Story Link

God's People

Have the children stand and sing this song with you to the tune of "If You're Happy and You Know It." Discuss how the Bible story tells us about God's people, the Jews. God gives his people important instructions to follow.

1st Verse:

> *If you're one of God's people march around.*
> *If you're one of God's people march around.*
> *If you're one of God's people, then you'll follow him and show it.*
> *If you're one of God's people march around.*

2nd Verse:

> *If you're one of God's people, blow your trumpet …*

3rd Verse:

> *If you're one of God's people shout, "For the Lord!" …*

Get List:
- None

Game

All Fall Down

Using two teams, line up each and have them grab hands, making a team wall. Have the two different lines face each other about 10 feet apart. Have one team start by shouting together, "For the Lord we loudly cry, send _____ (fill in a player's name from the other team) over to our side." The child's name who was called runs to the other side and tries to break through the arms of the other team. If the child breaks through, the whole team falls down. If the child doesn't break their arms apart, that child becomes part of their team wall. Teams take turns shouting the phrase and calling out names.

Get List:
- Crayons or washable markers
- Butcher paper or construction paper
- Optional: Scissors and glue

Extension Activity

Picturing God's Power

Allow the children to work in groups, or individually, to draw pictures of how big and powerful God is. Have the children explain what they drew. Remind them of the following after they present their pictures: **Because God is so big and so powerful, he used Joshua to bring down the walls of the city of Jericho. His way is always the best way.**

Soak It In
Bible Story Hands-on Activities

These activities can be used with large or small groups or as individual stations.

Get List:
- Paper plates
- Large marshmallows
- Graham crackers divided into fourths

Activity 1

Walls of Jericho

On a paper plate, the children will build walls using marshmallows and graham crackers. **Today we're going to learn how God brought the walls of Jericho tumbling down. Once you build your walls, you may knock them down and eat them!** *Note: Check with parents for food allergies.*

Get List:
- Construction paper
- Tape
- Scissors
- Streamers
- Markers

Activity 2

God's Winners

But thanks be to God! He gives us the victory through our Lord Jesus Christ. (1 Corinthians 15:57)

Have the children make winners' ribbons. Cut three-inch circles from construction paper. Cut eight-inch streamers. Tape three streamers to the back of the circle. Flip the winner's ribbon over. Help the children write the Bible reference, 1 Corinthians 15:57, on the circle. On each ribbon help them write one part of the Bible Verse. Make an example for the children to copy. Tell them when they're on God's side, they're winners.

Get List:
- Building blocks

Activity 3

Wall of Jericho

Have the children set up blocks in rows, like dominoes. Have them knock over the first block in its row. When they knock down the wall, have them shout, "Victory is the Lord's!" Watch the walls fall down. Tell them they'll learn how God and his people knocked down the walls of Jericho in the Bible story.

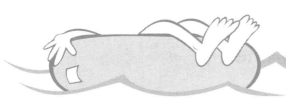

Soak It In
Bible Story Time

Get List:
- Bible
- Completed *Flippers Up* made from the reproducible page

Gather the children for story time. Be sure they have their *Flippers Up* ready to go. Hold up a Bible for the children to see. **To tell this story I'm going to need your help.** Divide the group in half, down the middle of the room. Point to the children on the left: **Whenever I raise my trumpet, you shout through your trumpet, "Victory is nigh!"** (Explain that the word nigh means near.) Then point to the children on the right: **Now, raise your trumpets and shout, "Is the Lord's battle cry!"** Have the children practice several times.

In the Bible in the book of Joshua, we learn how God helped his people conquer the city of Jericho (trumpet). A long time ago, the Jews, God's people, were taken away from their homeland. God decided it was time for the Jews to return to their land. God put Joshua in charge of taking the land back for God's people (trumpet).

To get the land back, God's people had to take the city of Jericho. But the city of Jericho was surrounded by a giant wall, the biggest city wall ever built. How were Joshua and God's people going to take back the city? God had a plan (trumpet).

God told Joshua to gather the people. He told them to march around the city once a day for six days. Then on the seventh day they were to march around the city seven times, blow their horns and shout. Would this plan really work? This didn't sound like a smart battle plan (trumpet).

Joshua and God's people did as God had said to do. On the seventh day they marched around the city seven times. Then they blew their horns and gave a big shout (trumpet). Do you know what happened next? God did an amazing thing. The city walls of Jericho came rumbling and tumbling down (trumpet). Now God's people could have their land and city back. This story shows us God is powerful and loves his people. The people did what God had said to do, because his ways are the right ways (trumpet).

- Why did the people march around the city of Jericho? *(that was the plan God gave Joshua for making the walls fall down)*
- Who had the power to make the walls of the city come tumbling down? *(God)*
- Who listened to God and led the people? *(Joshua)*

Sail Away

Get List:
- None

Prayer

Have the children form a circle, then have them march around in their circle formation one time. Have them tell you one thing they remember from the Bible story. Have them march in a circle again and ask them again what they remember. Do this seven times. After the seventh time, have everyone shout, "Victory is nigh, is the Lord's battle cry!" Then have all the children fall down. Lead the children in this prayer: **Dear God, thank you for being so powerful. Thank you for loving and caring for us. Help us to follow your ways, for your ways are the right ways. In Jesus' name, amen.**

Get List:
- None

Cleanup

Every time the children pick up an item while they are cleaning up, have them shout out, "Nothing is impossible with God!"

Get List:
- Completed *Flippers Up*
- Copy of *Home Connection* for each child

Homeward Bound

As the children leave, make sure they have their completed *Flippers Up* they made for Bible Story Time. As they leave, tell them their trumpets remind you of how God helped Joshua and the people conquer Jericho. Then have the children shout through their trumpets, "Victory is nigh, is the Lord's battle cry!"

- Who listened to God and followed his ways?
- Who is powerful?

PINT-SIZE BIBLE BITES

Joshua was one of only two adults who experienced Egyptian slavery and lived to enter the Promised Land; the other was Caleb.

TEACHER TIP

Wars or battles in the Bible are sometimes difficult to understand. One thing we do know: God wants what is best for his people. God had promised his people this special land and God fulfilled that promise.

Home Connection
Dive In!

Title: All Fall Down

Bible Story: Joshua 6:1–20

Bible Truth: God is powerful. His way is the right way.

Bible Verse: But thanks be to God! He gives us the victory through our Lord Jesus Christ. (1 Corinthians 15:57)

- In this lesson your child **heard** the story of how God used Joshua to bring down the walls of the city of Jericho.

- In this lesson your child **learned** that God loves and cares for his people.

- In this lesson your child **remembered** God is powerful and his way is the right way to do things.

In this Bible story, God's people were reclaiming the land that had once been theirs. Conquering the city of Jericho was God's way of restoring the Israelites to their homeland as he had promised. God did this in a truly unusual way. The people marched around the city for seven days, blew on trumpets and then shouted. Then the city walls of Jericho came tumbling down. God's ways may not always make sense to us, but we can be assured that God's ways are the right ways.

HOME CONNECTIONS

These are items used during the Bible story lesson that might be commonly found in your home. When your child sees or plays with one of the items mentioned below, help make the connection to the Bible story.

Horn: The trumpet or ram's horn was used in this Bible story. When you are in your car, beep your horn as your child shouts, "Victory is nigh, is the Lord's battle cry!"

Blocks: The blocks were used to build a wall, like dominoes. Then tip the first block over to make the others fall down. You can also build a wall of blocks with your child. Then talk about the Bible story of Joshua and the walls of Jericho.

KEEPING CONNECTED

Here are two simple activities that were used in class during the Bible story lesson, All Fall Down. Use these activities to help your child remember the Bible story lesson.

Walls of Jericho

Give your child large marshmallows and graham crackers. Have your child make a wall of Jericho with you. See how long or high you can build your wall. Or, knock it down and eat it together. Talk about how God helped Joshua and the people bring the walls of Jericho tumbling down.

God's People

Sing this song with your child to the tune of, "If You're Happy and You Know It":

1st Verse
> *If you're one of God's people march around. (2X)*
> *If you're one of God's people, then you'll follow him and show it,*
> *If you're one of God's people march around.*

2nd Verse
> *If you're one of God's people, blow your trumpet ...*

3rd Verse
> *If you're one of God's people shout, "For the Lord!" ...*

Prayer

Make a special ribbon for you child, and tell your child how special he or she is. As you tuck your little one into bed, give your child the ribbon. Then say this prayer: **Dear God, thank you for _____ (child's name). He/She is a winner to me. Help him/her to follow you. May _____ always remember that your way is the best way. In Jesus' name, amen.**

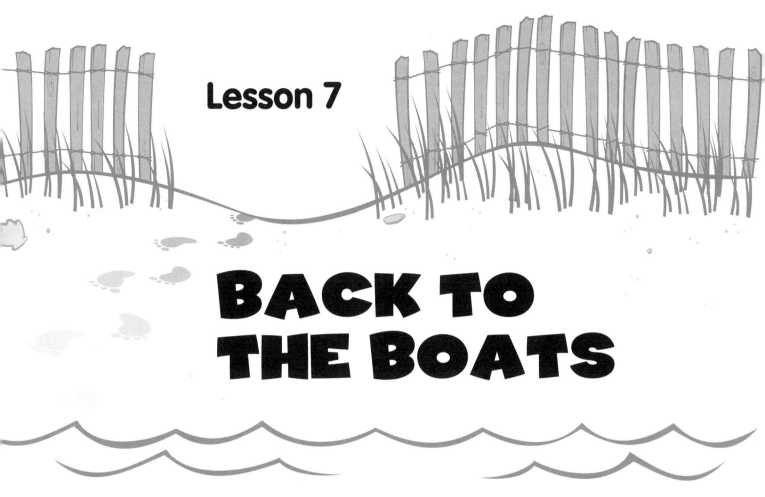

Lesson 7

BACK TO THE BOATS

Bible Story: John 21:1–17

Bible Truth: God forgives us.

Bible Verse: And the God of all grace … will himself restore you and make you strong, firm and steadfast. (1 Peter 5:10)

Children make mistakes all the time; it's part of learning and growing. Children need to learn that those mistakes may have consequences and could be life changing, but they can still be forgiven. Reinforce with your children that Jesus Christ is always ready to forgive.

- In this lesson children will **hear** how Jesus forgave Peter and encouraged Peter to follow him.

- In this lesson children will **learn** that sin and mistakes can be forgiven by Jesus.

- In this lesson children will **remember** that Jesus forgives us.

LESSON SEVEN SNAPSHOT

Flippers Up
Reproducible Page

- [ ] Copies of page 57 for each child
- [ ] Scissors
- [ ] Crayons or markers
- [ ] Straws
- [ ] Tape or stapler

Splash-n-Spray

Bible Story Link:
Jump in the Boat
- [ ] Masking tape

Game:
Full Nets
- [ ] Fishnet (can also use shower curtain, blanket or bed sheet)
- [ ] 20 balloons
- [ ] Permanent marker

Extension Activity:
Forgive and Forget
- [ ] Index cards
- [ ] Pens or markers

Soak It In
Bible Story
Hands-on Activities

Activity 1:
Breakfast on the Beach
- [ ] Beach towels
- [ ] Toaster
- [ ] Paper plates
- [ ] Round waffles
- [ ] Optional: Syrup

Activity 2:
Beach Ball Bible Memory
- [ ] Beach ball

Activity 3:
Jesus Floats Our Boats
- [ ] Tub of water
- [ ] Game cube
- [ ] Small foam cups, one per child
- [ ] Scissors
- [ ] Pennies

Bible Story Time
- [ ] Bible
- [ ] Completed *Flippers Up* made from the reproducible page

Sail Away

Prayer
- [ ] Beach towel

Cleanup
- [ ] Several beach towels

Homeward Bound
- [ ] Completed *Flippers Up*
- [ ] Copy of *Home Connection* from page 62 for each child

HEART OF THE STORY

Peter loved Jesus, but he denied Jesus three times. He felt terrible about doing this. Everything changed for the better when Jesus reappeared that morning on the beach. Jesus asked Peter, "Do you love me?" Jesus wanted to know if he loved him completely. Peter realized that he truly did not, or he wouldn't have denied Jesus three times on the eve of his crucifixion. Jesus asked Peter three times if he loved him in order to restore Peter to himself. Although Peter admitted he had not loved Jesus completely, Jesus totally forgave him and told him to follow him.

If Jesus asked if you love him completely, what would you say? Would you lay down your life for him?

Flippers Up
Bible Story Reproducible Page

Get List:
- A copy of the reproducible on this page for each child
- Scissors
- Crayons or markers
- Straws
- Tape or stapler

Have the children color the pictures. Cut out the bottom part of the boat. Fold on the dotted lines. Punch a hole where indicated. Cut out the sails and tape or staple to a straw. Set up the boat and place the straw through the center hole in the boat. Turn the straw to flip the sail from one side to the other.

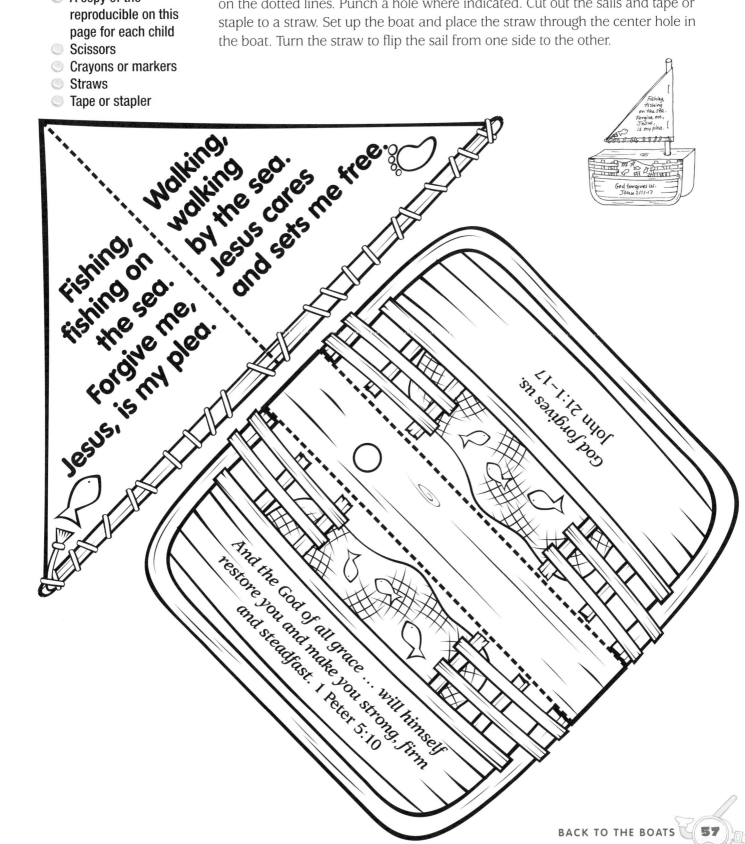

Fishing, fishing on the sea. Forgive me, Jesus, is my plea.

Walking, walking by the sea. Jesus cares and sets me free.

God forgives us. John 21:1-17

And the God of all grace ... will himself restore you and make you strong, firm and steadfast. 1 Peter 5:10

Splash-n-Spray

Use these *Splash-n-Spray* activities to build knowledge that enriches the children's experience with the lesson while having fun.

Get List:
- Masking tape

Bible Story Link

Jump in the Boat
Tape the outline shape of a boat on the floor. Be sure it's big enough for all the children to fit into. Begin by having all the children stand outside the boat. Ask a question that always starts: "If you have ever _____, jump in the boat." Start with simple things, then eventually move to things that might cause children to get into trouble, such as fight with a sibling, lie, not do chores, etc. Help them see that we've all done things that hurt Jesus' heart, just like Peter hurt Jesus' heart in the Bible story.

Get List:
- Fishnet (can also use shower curtain, blanket or bed sheet)
- 20 balloons
- Permanent marker

Game

Full Nets
Inflate the balloons and draw fish on 12 of them. Start the game by having the children hold the edges of the net. Toss all the balloons onto the net. Have the children raise the net up and down to try to keep only the fish balloons on the net. See how many fish fill their net at the end of a designated time period.

Get List:
- Index cards
- Pens or markers

Extension Activity

Forgive and Forget
This is just like the classic matching card game. You can choose to draw the pictures on one side of all the index cards beforehand or have children draw them during class. Remember, there should be two of each card! The pictures should be simple drawings of different things that we have all done wrong (fighting with a sibling, lying, not doing chores, eating too many cookies before dinner, etc.). Some could even be as simple as a sad face. On the other side of every card draw a cross (must all be identical) to represent Jesus forgiving us. Lay all the cards down on the table with the cross sides facing up. Each child will get an opportunity to turn over two cards, trying to find a match. Tell the children, **Sometimes when we play this game, it's hard to remember. We forget. When Jesus forgives us, it is sort of like that. He forgets the wrong things we've done because he loves us.**

Soak It In

Bible Story Hands-on Activities

These activities can be used with large or small groups or as individual stations.

Get List:
- Beach towels
- Toaster
- Paper plates
- Round waffles
- Optional: Syrup

Activity 1

Breakfast on the Beach

Have the children sit on beach towels. Toast the waffles and distribute the plates. Each child needs one full, round waffle and one half-waffle. Place the whole waffle on the plate first with the rounded side of the half-waffle against it to make the fish tail. Discuss how Jesus had breakfast on the beach with the disciples, and they ate bread and fish. *Note: Check with parents for food allergies.*

Get List:
- Beach ball

Activity 2

Beach Ball Bible Memory

And the God of all grace … will himself restore you and make you strong, firm and steadfast. (1 Peter 5:10)

Start by hitting the beach ball in the air. The children should try to keep the ball in the air as long as possible. If it falls to the ground, everyone must freeze and say the Bible Verse together. Begin again, trying to keep the ball in the air.

Get List:
- Tub of water
- Game cube
- Small foam cups, one per child
- Scissors
- Pennies

Activity 3

Jesus Floats Our Boats

Cut the cups to a 1½-inch height. Fill the tub with water. Place the boats (cups) in the water. Have the children roll the game cube. The number rolled is the number of pennies added to their boat. They keep rolling and adding pennies until their boats sink. **These pennies are just like sin in our lives. Sin can sink our boats! In today's Bible story, Peter had sinned against Jesus. But Jesus forgave Peter. When Jesus forgives us, it's like he takes all our pennies away. His forgiveness keeps our boats afloat.**

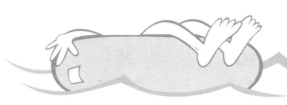

Soak It In
Bible Story Time

Get List:
- Bible
- Completed *Flippers Up* made from the reproducible page

Gather the children for story time. Be sure they have their *Flippers Up* ready to go. Hold up a Bible for the children to see. Tell the children that when you say "fish" they flip their sails to show the fish and say together, "Fishing, fishing on the sea. Forgive me, Jesus, is my plea." When you say "footprints," have the children flip to the sail with the footprint and say together, "Walking, walking by the sea. Jesus cares and sets me free."

The Bible, in the book of John, tells us about a time when Peter, who was one of Jesus' disciples, really learned that Jesus forgives us. Peter did something wrong. Have you ever done something wrong?

Peter was sad about what he did, and he knew it was wrong. He probably thought about it a lot.

One night, Peter and some other disciples, went fishing. They were out on the sea in their boats, but they weren't catching anything, and maybe Peter wasn't even thinking about fish. (have children flip their sails to show the fish and say with you ...) **Fishing, fishing on the sea. Forgive me, Jesus, is my plea.**

You are right! Peter was wanting Jesus to forgive him.

Peter and the disciples fished all night in the dark and didn't catch anything. They stayed out on the sea so long that the night became the next morning and the sun came up. Peter was probably still not thinking about fish. *(flip sails to show the fish and say: Fishing, fishing on the sea. Forgive me, Jesus, is my plea)*

With the daylight, the disciples saw a man walking on the beach. He asked what they caught and the disciples answered, "Nothing". The man told them to put their fishing net on the other side of the boat. Suddenly the net was full of fish. *(flip sails to show the fish and say: Fishing, fishing on the sea. Forgive me, Jesus, is my plea)* **Thanks for the reminder! The full net helped the disciples realize the man on the beach was Jesus.**

Peter was so excited he jumped out of the boat—but he didn't make a footprint. (have children flip their sails to show the footprint and say with you: walking, walking by the sea. Jesus cares and sets me free) **Peter didn't make a footprint because he stepped into the water.**

Peter and the other disciples made it to shore where Jesus had breakfast ready for them. They all ate, but Peter also looked at the sand and saw footprints. *(flip sails to show the footprints and say walking, walking by the sea. Jesus cares and sets me free)*

Jesus and Peter talked. Jesus forgave Peter and also told Peter to keep following him. Peter was so happy because he knew Jesus had forgiven him. Jesus forgives us too.

- Who did something wrong? *(Peter)*
- Who forgave Peter and set him free? *(Jesus)*
- Who forgives you? *(Jesus)*

Sail Away

Get List:
- Beach towel

Prayer

Hold up a beach towel. Tell the children the beach towel reminds you of the breakfast Jesus had with the disciples on the beach. Pass the towel around. As you pass it, have the children tell you something they remember from the Bible story. Then lead them in this prayer: **Dear God, thank you for loving us and caring for us. Thank you for Jesus who can forgive us of the things we do wrong. Help us to follow Jesus. In Jesus' name, amen.**

Get List:
- Several beach towels

Cleanup

Have the children use beach towels to gather up their things as they clean. As they clean, repeat this phrase, "Cleaning, cleaning by the sea. Jesus cares and sets us free."

Get List:
- Completed *Flippers Up*
- Copy of *Home Connection* for each child

Homeward Bound

As the children prepare to leave, make sure they have their completed *Flippers Up* they made for Bible Story Time. As they leave, have them point to the fish side of their sail. See if they can remember the phrase on it. Do the same with the other side of the sail. Say the phrases with them.

- Who can forgive you and set you free?
- Who can keep your boat afloat?

PINT-SIZE BIBLE BITES

The Sea of Galilee is actually a freshwater lake. It is known by three other names—Sea of Chinnereth, Lake of Gennesaret and Sea of Tiberias.

TEACHER TIP

Some children will associate accidents such as dropping and breaking something as sin. Be sure to clarify that sin is when we purposefully hurt God's heart by making a choice that is against what he would want us to.

Home Connection
Dive In!

Title: Back to the Boats

Bible Story: John 21:1–17

Bible Truth: God forgives us.

Bible Verse: And the God of all grace … will himself restore you and make you strong, firm and steadfast. (1 Peter 5:10)

- In this lesson your child **heard** how Jesus forgave Peter and encouraged Peter to follow him.
- In this lesson your child **learned** that sin and mistakes can be forgiven by Jesus.
- In this lesson your child **remembered** that Jesus forgives us.

In this Bible story, the disciples are fishing when Jesus appears on the beach. This is Jesus' third appearance after his resurrection. Jesus and the disciples end up having breakfast together on the beach. After breakfast Jesus and Peter talk. Jesus forgives Peter for denying him and encourages Peter to follow him. When your child sins, be sure to reassure your child that sins are forgiven by Jesus.

HOME CONNECTIONS

These are items used during the Bible story lesson that might be commonly found in your home. When your child sees or plays with one of the items mentioned below, help make the connection to the Bible story.

Boat: In this Bible story, the disciples were in their fishing boat when Jesus called out to them. The next time your child plays with a boat, remind him or her of the time when Jesus had breakfast with the disciples on the beach.

Beach towel: A beach towel was used to remind the children that Jesus had breakfast with the disciples on the beach. Surprise your child some morning with breakfast on a beach towel. Then talk about the Bible story.

KEEPING CONNECTED

Here are two simple activities that were used in class during the Bible story lesson, Back to the Boats. Use these activities to help your child remember the Bible story lesson.

Breakfast on the Beach

Have a special beach breakfast with your child. Lay out a beach towel. Toast round waffles. Place one round waffle on a plate. Cut another waffle in half, and place it next to the round waffle to make a tail for the fish. You could add a syrup smile and a chocolate chip eye. Discuss how Jesus had breakfast on the beach with the disciples, and that they ate bread and fish.

Jesus Floats Our Boats

Cut a foam cup to a 1½-inch height. Fill a tub with water. Place the boat (cup) in the water. Have your child roll a game cube. The number rolled is the number of pennies to add to the boat. Keep rolling and adding pennies until the boat sinks. Explain how the pennies are like sin in our lives. Sin can sink our boats. In the Bible story, Peter had sinned against Jesus. When Jesus forgives us, like he forgave Peter, he takes all our sins away. Jesus' forgiveness can always keep our boats afloat.

Prayer

Surprise your child with bedtime on the beach before getting tucked into bed. Roll out a beach towel then read books or play a game together. Talk about the Bible story. Close your time with this prayer: **Dear God, thank you for forgiving us when we do something wrong. Help us make good choices. Thank you for loving us. In Jesus' name, amen.**

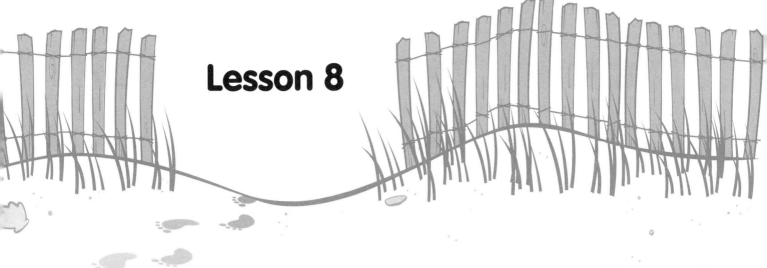

Lesson 8

JUST SAY YES!

Bible Story: Jonah 1—4

Bible Truth: God wants me to obey him.

Bible Verse: You are my portion, O LORD; I have promised to obey your words. (Psalm 119:57)

Splish, splash flops the huge fish. The story of Jonah and the great fish makes for a whale of a tale. Make sure the children grab onto the truth of saying yes to God. It's always best to follow God's ways.

- In this lesson children will **hear** the story of Jonah and the great big fish.

- In this lesson children will **learn** that it's best to obey God.

- In this lesson children will **remember** to obey God and follow his ways.

LESSON EIGHT SNAPSHOT

Flippers Up
Reproducible Page

- [ ] Copies of page 65 for each child
- [x] Crayons or markers
- [ ] Metal brads
- [ ] Scissors

Splash-n-Spray

Bible Story Link:
Show Me
- [ ] None

Game:
The Obey Game
- [ ] None

Extension Activity:
Jonah Jingle
- [ ] None

Soak It In
Bible Story
Hands-on Activities

Activity 1:
Great Big Fish
- [ ] Blue gelatin
- [ ] Gummy fish
- [ ] Clear plastic cups (one per child)
- [ ] Spoons (one per child)

Activity 2:
Splish-Splash Fish
- [ ] 2 buckets of water
- [ ] Several small sponges
- [ ] Scissors
- [ ] Masking tape

Activity 3:
Fishy Art
- [ ] Paper plates (two per child)
- [ ] Scissors
- [ ] Tempera paint
- [ ] Sponge pieces (left from Splish-Splash Fish)
- [ ] Black marker

Bible Story Time
- [ ] Bible
- [ ] Completed *Flippers Up* made from the reproducible page

Sail Away

Prayer
- [ ] Blanket

Cleanup
- [ ] None

Homeward Bound
- [ ] Completed *Flippers Up*
- [ ] Copy of *Home Connection* from page 70 for each child

HEART OF THE STORY

Have you ever despised someone or felt a person was so evil you believed that person was beyond redemption? That's how Jonah felt about the people of Nineveh. Jonah knew the message of God would transform and redeem them. He believed they had been so evil they didn't deserve God's redemption. Sometimes it's hard to just say yes. When Jonah finally did go to Nineveh, he turned a city of 120,000 people to follow God. God can use the most reluctant people to do his work. Let your little ones know, God is truly a God of mercy, forgiveness and redemption, which none of us really deserves.

Flippers Up
Bible Story Reproducible Page

Get List:
- A copy of the reproducible on this page for each child
- Crayons or markers
- Metal brads
- Scissors

Have children color the great fish. Cut out the fish parts. Attach the mouth and tail with metal brads. Show the children how the fish's mouth moves like a puppet.

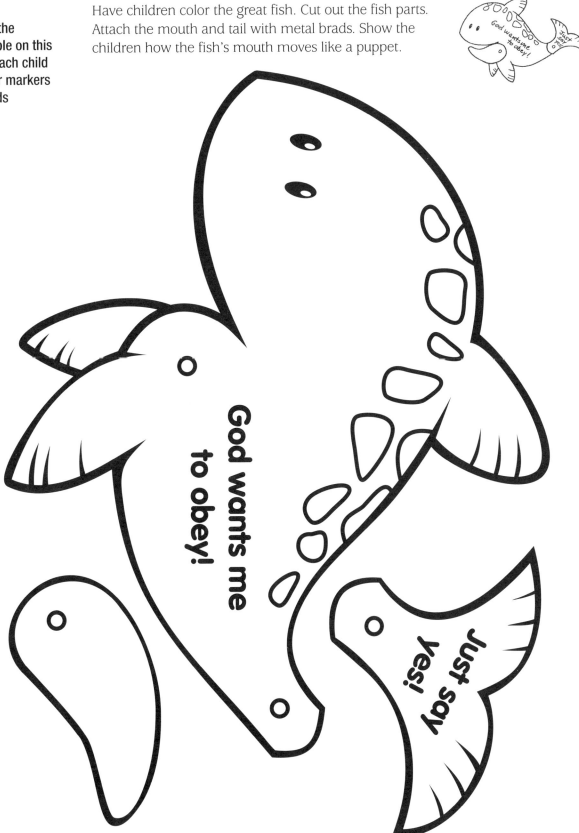

God wants me to obey!

Just say yes!

Splash-n-Spray

Use these *Splash-n-Spray* activities to build knowledge that enriches the children's experience with the lesson while having fun.

Get List:
None

Show Me

Have the children show you the opposite of what you command. Start by saying, **Do you know the opposite of sit, run and stop?** Allow time for answers. Then have the children go in the opposite direction you point. Discuss times when someone told you to do something and you did the opposite. Ask if the children have any opposite stories to share. **Today we're going to learn about a man named Jonah, who did the opposite of what God told him to do.**

Get List:
None

The Obey Game

Gather all the children to one side of the room, while you stand on the other side. Tell them they are to obey what you say. If they don't obey right away, they have to start all over. The first child to reach you is the winner. Call out different commands, such as walk, hop, skip, jump or run. Then tell them to freeze or stop. Intermix the action commands with the freeze or stop commands. Send children back to the start line if they don't immediately obey.

Get List:
None

Jonah Jingle

Sing this song about Jonah to the tune of *Jingle Bells*. Encourage children to follow your motions (change them after a few times for a challenge), as Jonah should have followed God.

In the fish, in the fish, (hands over head)
It is dark in here. (squat down)
Should have done just what God said, (point up)
But I went my own way-ay. (stand and march to the left)
In the fish, in the fish, (hands over head)
I'll kneel down and pray. (kneel, fold hands as if praying)
Because it isn't any good (shake head)
Unless I walk God's way. (stand up and march to right)

Soak It In

Bible Story Hands-on Activities

These activities can be used with large or small groups or as individual stations.

Get List:
- Blue gelatin
- Gummy fish
- Clear plastic cups (one per child)
- Spoons (one per child)

Great Big Fish

Make and chill blue gelatin according to package directions. Scoop gelatin into small, clear plastic cups. Add one gummy fish to each cup. Have the children look for the fish in their cups. As they eat, talk about how they will learn about a man named Jonah who was swallowed by a great big fish. *Note: Check with parents for any food allergies.*

Get List:
- 2 buckets of water
- Several small sponges
- Scissors
- Masking tape

Splish-Splash Fish

You are my portion, O LORD; I have promised to obey your words. (Psalm 119:57)

Tape a six-foot circle on the floor. Place one bucket of water in the center of the circle and one bucket of water outside of the circle. (Empty buckets may also be used.) Cut the small sponges into fish shapes. Place the sponge fish in the bucket outside of the circle. Have the children stand outside the circle and toss the sponges into the center bucket. They can retrieve any sponges that didn't make it into the bucket, but they must always toss from outside the circle. When they make it into the bucket have everyone shout the Bible Verse.

Get List:
- Paper plates
- Scissors
- Tempera paint
- Sponge pieces (left from Splish-Splash Fish)
- Black marker

Fishy Art

Cut a fish shape from a paper plate. Use this to trace a fish shape onto a paper plate for each child. Have the children use the leftover sponge pieces (from the previous activity) to paint their fish by dipping them in tempera paint and sponging them onto their paper plate fish. Use a black marker to draw the figure of Jonah on the back of the plate. When you hold up the fish to a light, you should be able to see Jonah in the belly of the fish.

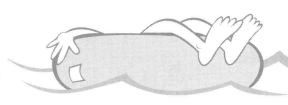

Soak It In
Bible Story Time

Get List:
- Bible
- Completed *Flippers Up* made from the reproducible page

Gather the children for story time. Be sure they have their *Flippers Up* ready to go. Hold a Bible for the children to see. **Everyone hold up your fish when I move my hands like this …** (cup your hands together one on top of the other, then open and shut them). **You and your fish will say, "Jonah listen and obey, you must follow God's way."** Have children practice.

In the Bible, in the book of Jonah, there's a story about a man named Jonah. **God told Jonah to go to a city called Nineveh** (hands). **The people in the city of Nineveh were doing bad things. God wanted Jonah to go there and tell the people to follow God's ways** (hands). **Jonah did not like the people of Nineveh. He decided not to go there, so he got in a boat and went in the opposite direction** (hands).

Jonah did not follow God's way. Jonah decided to do things his way, and this got him into some big trouble. While Jonah was on the boat, a great storm blew in. It tossed the boat around. Jonah thought he should have listened to God (hands). Jonah knew he had made a bad choice. Jonah told the sailors on the boat that the reason there was a bad storm was because he knew he went the wrong way (hands).

Jonah made the sailors toss him into the sea. Jonah splished and splashed and was beginning to sink to the bottom of the sea, when all of a sudden a large fish swallowed him up. Now Jonah was not sinking in the sea; he was in the belly of the great big fish (hands).

Jonah was in the belly of the fish for three days and three nights. Jonah had time to do a lot of thinking. Jonah was thinking he should follow God's way (hands). When Jonah finally got out of the belly of the fish, he did what God had asked him and went to the city of Nineveh (hands). While in Nineveh, he told the people about God. God was very happy Jonah finally obeyed (hands).

- **Why was Jonah in the belly of a fish?** *(he didn't follow God's way)*
- **Whose way should Jonah have followed?** *(God's)*
- **Who should you obey?** *(God)*

Sail Away

Get List:
- Blanket

Prayer

Have the children gather under a blanket with you. Pretend you are all in the belly of the fish. Ask the children questions about the Bible story. If the question has to do with Jonah following God, then everyone can get out of the fish's belly. If the question has to do with Jonah's disobedience, you must all stay in or return to the belly of the fish. Then lead the children in this prayer: **Dear God, help us to follow you. We love you and want to obey you. We want to do things your way. In Jesus' name, amen.**

Get List:
- None

Cleanup

As the children clean up, lead them in this cheer: **Give me an O.** Have the children respond with O. **Give me a B. Give me an E. Give me a Y. What's this spell? OBEY.** Have the children chant and repeat: "We will obey, yeah!"

Get List:
- Completed *Flippers Up*
- Copy of *Home Connection* for each child

Homeward Bound

As the children leave, make sure they have their completed *Flippers Up* they made for Bible Story Time. Have them spell the word *obey* for you. Then tell them you learned that obey means to do what God wants us to do.

- What does obey mean to you?
- Did Jonah obey God?

PINT-SIZE BIBLE BITES

Jonah is the only prophetic book in the Bible that focuses on a story, and not on prophecies. Jesus also mentions this story.

TEACHER TIP

Obedience at any age can be difficult. Emphasize to the children that obedience is an act of love. Point out to them that even when they don't want to obey, like Jonah, they can still choose to obey. And by obeying, they say, "I love you God."

Home Connection
Dive In!

Title: Just Say Yes!

Bible Story: Jonah 1—4

Bible Truth: God wants me to obey him.

Bible Verse: You are my portion, O LORD; I have promised to obey your words. (Psalm 119:57)

- In this lesson your child **heard** the story of Jonah and the great big fish.
- In this lesson your child **learned** that it's best to obey God.
- In this lesson your child **remembered** to obey God and follow his ways.

In this Bible story, God tells Jonah to go to the city of Nineveh to preach to the people. Jonah didn't want to go to Nineveh, so he got on a boat and went in the opposite direction God wanted him to go. Needless to say, this didn't work out for Jonah. He ended up in the belly of a great fish. This gave him plenty of time to change his mind and obey God. Teach your little ones it is so much easier on us if we obey God and do what is right.

HOME CONNECTIONS

These are items used during the Bible story lesson that might be commonly found in your home. When your child sees or plays with one of the items mentioned below, help make the connection to the Bible story.

Sponges: Sponges were used to make fish for a game. When you use a sponge at home, soak up some water in it and wring the water out. Talk about how the sponge reminds you of Jonah in the sea. God sent a great big fish to swallow Jonah. Jonah learned to obey God.

Fish: Fish were used throughout the lesson. When you see a fish or have fish for dinner, discuss the huge fish in the Bible story of Jonah. Jonah was in the belly of the fish for three days and nights.

KEEPING CONNECTED

Here are two simple activities that were used in class during the Bible story lesson, Just Say Yes! Use these activities to help your child remember the Bible story lesson.

Show Me

Just for fun, have your child show you the opposite of what you command. Start by saying, **Do you know the opposite of sit, run and stop?** Talk about a time when someone told you to do something and you did the opposite. Then talk about how Jonah did the opposite of what God asked him to do, but later found out it was best to obey God and do what is right.

Great Big Fish

Make blue gelatin according to package directions. Pour gelatin into a large pan, then cut out a large fish shape. Enjoy eating the big fish with your child. Talk about how Jonah ended up in the belly of a fish because he didn't obey God. In the end, Jonah did what God had asked him to do.

Prayer

Children love to listen to stories. Talk about a time when someone asked you to do something and you did the opposite. Discuss what you learned from your experience. Then discuss how you felt as you made your choices. Ask if your child has a story to talk about too. Then lead your child in this prayer: **Dear God, thank you for loving us and giving us second chances. Please help us to obey you and do what is right. In Jesus' name, amen.**

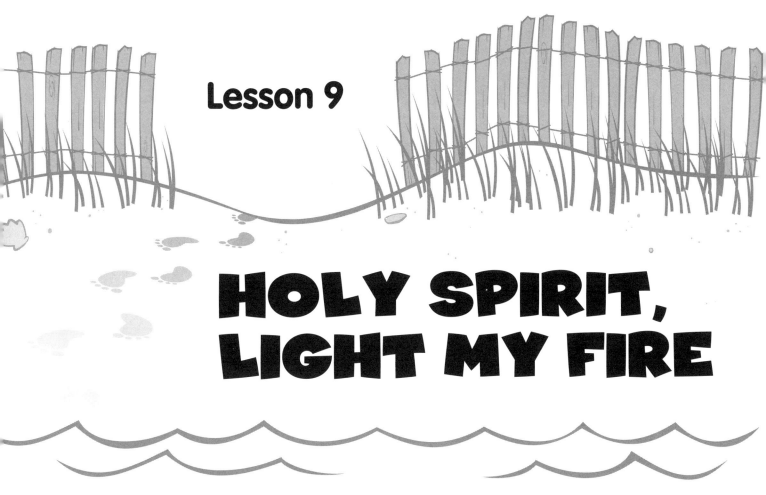

Lesson 9

HOLY SPIRIT, LIGHT MY FIRE

Bible Story: Acts 2:1–12

Bible Truth: God is with us.

Bible Verse: But you will receive power when the Holy Spirit comes on you. (Acts 1:8)

Many children and adults struggle with feeling powerless and lonely sometimes. Be ready to see the children light up as they discover how God, through his Holy Spirit, is always with them. With God all things are possible, and we are never alone.

◉ In this lesson children will **hear** the story of Pentecost.

◉ In this lesson children will **learn** that during Pentecost, God gave us his Holy Spirit.

◉ In this lesson children will **remember** God is always with us.

LESSON NINE SNAPSHOT

Flippers Up
Reproducible Page

- [ ] Copies of page 73 for each child
- [x] Scissors
- [ ] Tape
- [ ] Crayons or markers

Splash-n-Spray

Bible Story Link:
How Do You Say Hello?
- [ ] Index cards
- [ ] Marker

Game:
Light My Fire
- [ ] Empty paper towel rolls
- [ ] Tape
- [ ] Red or orange tissue paper

Extension Activity:
Power Bracelets
- [ ] Black elastic (1/2" wide)
- [ ] Large, red, orange and yellow beads

Soak It In
Bible Story
Hands-on Activities

Activity 1:
Power Bars
- [ ] Graham crackers
- [ ] Chocolate bars
- [ ] Marshmallow crème
- [ ] Craft sticks
- [ ] Bowls
- [ ] Paper plates

Activity 2:
Light My Bible Verse
- [ ] Copy paper
- [ ] Markers
- [ ] Tape
- [ ] Flashlights

Activity 3:
Pente-cost
- [ ] Lots of pennies
- [ ] Game cube
- [ ] Paper
- [ ] Marker

Bible Story Time
- [ ] Bible
- [ ] Completed *Flippers Up* made from the reproducible page

Sail Away

Prayer
- [ ] Torch made from tissue paper and empty paper towel roll

Cleanup
- [ ] None

Homeward Bound
- [ ] Completed *Flippers Up*
- [ ] Copy of *Home Connection* from page 78 for each child

HEART OF THE STORY

Jesus had died and ascended into heaven. Ten days after his ascension was the yearly festival called Pentecost or Feast of Weeks. Jews from all over gathered for this feast. Jesus' followers were anxiously waiting for God to send his Holy Spirit as Jesus had promised to do. The Holy Spirit came in a powerful demonstration that couldn't be missed by anyone. God's presence was now available to all who believed in him. Be excited with your little ones as they learn about God—who is with them every day.

Flippers Up
Bible Story Reproducible Page

Get List:
- A copy of the reproducible on this page for each child
- Scissors
- Tape
- Crayons or markers

Have the children color their Holy Spirit headbands. Cut out the headbands. Tape the two strips together to fit each child's head.

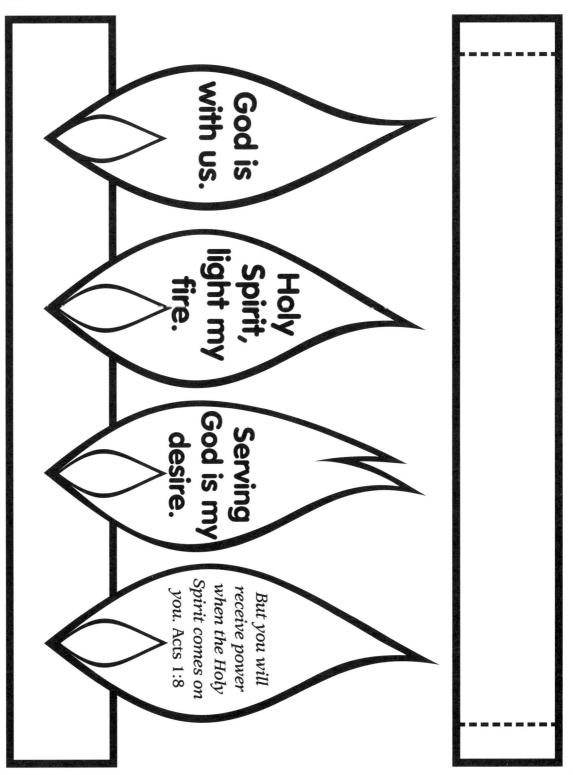

God is with us.

Holy Spirit, light my fire.

Serving God is my desire.

But you will receive power when the Holy Spirit comes on you. Acts 1:8

Splash-n-Spray

Use these *Splash-n-Spray* activities to build knowledge that enriches the children's experience with the lesson while having fun.

Get List:
- Index cards
- Marker

Bible Story Link

How Do You Say Hello?

On six different index cards write one of the following: hello (English), hola [o-la] (Spanish), guten tag [goot-en taug] (German), bonjour [bon-jur] (French), shalom [sha-lom] (Hebrew) and konnichiwa [ko-ne-che-wah] (Japanese). **In our Bible story today, people gathered from all over the world and spoke different languages. On these cards are six different ways to say hello in other languages.** Practice saying the words together. **When I show you a card, say "hello" to each other in that language and shake hands.**

Get List:
- Empty paper towel rolls
- Tape
- Red or orange tissue paper

Game

Light My Fire

Make a torch by taping a ball of tissue paper to the end of an empty paper-towel roll. Each team will need its own torch to play the relay game. Or, use one torch for a large group. Tape a start line on one side of the room and a goal line on the other side. Have the children form a long line along the start line. The first player runs to the goal line, then back to the start line and passes off the torch to the second player. Each time the torch is passed, the players must say, "Light my fire." Players keep advancing to the next player's spot as the torch is passed.

Get List:
- Black elastic (1/2" wide)
- Large red, orange and yellow beads

Extension Activity

Power Bracelets

Give each child a length of black elastic, tying a knot in one end. Place the colorful beads in several bowls around the table so all the children can reach them. While the children string the beads, tell them that the red, orange and yellow colors can remind them of the fire of the Holy Spirit at Pentecost. When they are done stringing the beads, tie the bracelets around their wrists. **You can wear your bracelet on your wrist and it can go anywhere with you. The Holy Spirit is like that. The Holy Spirit and his power will be with you wherever you go.**

Soak It In
Bible Story Hands-on Activities

These activities can be used with large or small groups or as individual stations.

Get List:
- Graham crackers
- Chocolate bars
- Marshmallow crème
- Craft sticks
- Bowls
- Paper plates

Power Bars

Give each child a paper plate. Place the items in bowls. Use the craft sticks for spreading. Have the children make their power bars by layering graham crackers, pieces of chocolate bar and marshmallow crème. Discuss with them how snacks fill us up with good things to give us energy, and how the Holy Spirit fills us with power from God. *Note: Check with parents for any food allergies.*

Get List:
- Copy paper
- Markers
- Tape
- Flashlights

Activity 2

Light My Bible Verse

But you will receive power when the Holy Spirit comes on you. (Acts 1:8)

Write parts of the Bible Verse on pieces of paper and tape the words around the room in an incorrect order. Have the children use flashlights to light up each word in the correct order of the Bible Verse as they say it aloud. Have them say "power on" each time they turn on the flashlight.

Get List:
- Lots of pennies
- Game cube
- Paper
- Marker

Activity 3

Pente-cost

Make a chart for a game cube. The children will roll a game cube to determine how many pennies they either collect or give back. Start with a large pile of pennies. If they roll a 1, 3 or 4 they must collect that number of pennies. If they roll a 2 or 5 they must give back that many pennies to the pile. If they roll a 6 they can make a choice to either collect that many pennies or put that many pennies back. The person who gets exactly 5 pennies first wins. Talk about how they will learn about a festival called Pentecost. The word *Pente* means "five," the number of pennies they need to win. (*Pentecost* means "fiftieth" in Greek.)

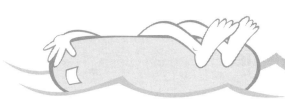

Soak It In
Bible Story Time

Get List:
- Bible
- Completed *Flippers Up* made from the reproducible page

Gather the children for story time. Be sure they have their *Flippers Up* ready to go. Have the children put on their Holy Spirit headbands. **Anytime you hear the word *Holy*, respond by holding up your flames and saying, "Spirit light my fire. Serving God is my desire."** Hold up a Bible for the children to see.

In the Bible in the book of Acts, we learn how God's people are on fire because of the Holy … (headbands).

There were many people from faraway lands who were gathered together for a feast called Pentecost. If you walked through the streets during Pentecost, you would hear people speaking many different languages. Jesus' disciples were at this feast too. The disciples were waiting for the Holy … (headbands).

Suddenly, the house shook with a great wind. It was a wind like they'd never heard before. It blew through the house like a tornado. Everyone was wondering what was happening. Could this be what God's people were waiting for? Could this be the Holy … (headbands).

The next moment there were flames of fire in the air. The flames settled on each of the disciples. And they were filled with the Holy … (headbands).

Then all at once the disciples started talking. But they were talking in all different kinds of languages that they didn't even know. All the people gathered for the festival were amazed. They could each understand what the disciples were saying in their own language. God was with his people through his Holy … (headbands).

More than 3,000 people believed in Jesus that day. God's Spirit helped the disciples tell others about Jesus. Long ago, at the feast of Pentecost, God gave us his Holy … (headbands).

- Why were all the people gathered together? *(to celebrate Pentecost)*
- Who gave us his Holy Spirit? *(God)*
- How do you know that God is with us? *(he gave us his Holy Spirit at Pentecost)*

Sail Away

Get List:
- Torch made from tissue paper ball and empty paper towel roll

Prayer
Pass the torch around. As you pass the torch, have the children tell you something they remember from the Bible story. Then lead the children in this prayer: **Dear God, thank you for being with us. Thank you for giving us your Holy Spirit to help us. We love you. In Jesus' name, amen.**

Get List:
- None

Cleanup
As the children clean up, see if they can remember how to say hello to each other in different languages. They can repeat the phrase, "Hi … Ho … _____ (form of word hello), God loves you so."

Get List:
- Completed *Flippers Up*
- Copy of *Home Connection* for each child

Homeward Bound
As the children leave, make sure they have their completed *Flippers Up* they made for Bible Story Time. Have the children show you their flames. Tell them their flames remind you of the Holy Spirit and how God is always with them.

- What do your flames remind you of?
- Who is always with you?

PINT-SIZE BIBLE BITES
Pentecost is one of three big Jewish festivals that are celebrated each year. Pentecost occurs 50 days after Passover and 10 days after Jesus' ascension. It is a type of "Thanksgiving Day" in celebration of the wheat harvest.

TEACHER TIP
There are a lot of abstract concepts taught in this Bible story. Try to focus on concrete ways of presenting these concepts while staying centered on the Bible truth—God is with us.

Home Connection
Dive In!

Title: Holy Spirit, Light My Fire

Bible Story: Acts 2:1–12

Bible Truth: God is with us.

Bible Verse: But you will receive power when the Holy Spirit comes on you. (Acts 1:8)

- In this lesson your child **heard** the story of Pentecost.
- In this lesson your child **learned** that during Pentecost God gave us his Holy Spirit.
- In this lesson your child **remembered** God is always with us.

In biblical times Pentecost was a festival that many people attended. In fact, people came from all over the world to attend. It was during this festival that God sent his Holy Spirit in a very dramatic way. The lives of many people changed on that day. Reinforce with your child that God is always with us because he gave us his Holy Spirit.

HOME CONNECTION

These are items used during the Bible story lesson that might be commonly found in your home. When your child sees or plays with one of the items mentioned below, help make the connection to the Bible story.

Fire: Fire was discussed throughout the Bible story lesson. The next time you light a fire, repeat this phrase to your child, **"Holy Spirit light my fire. Serving God is my desire."**

Flashlight: Your child used a flashlight to shine on different portions of the Bible Verse (see above). Each time you use a flashlight, tell your child it reminds you of the Bible story of Pentecost when God gave us the Holy Spirit.

KEEPING CONNECTED

Here are two simple activities that were used in class during the Bible story lesson, Holy Spirit, Light My Fire. Use these activities to help your child remember the Bible story lesson.

How Do You Say Hello?

On six different cards write one of the following: hello (English), hola (Spanish), guten tag (German), bonjour (French), shalom (Hebrew) and konnichiwa (Japanese). Explain these are different ways to say hello in other languages. Try to use these different ways of saying hello throughout your week. They should remind your child of how the Holy Spirit helped God's people spread his Word throughout the world during Pentecost by knowing different languages.

Pente-cost

Play the Pente-cost game. Start with a large pile of pennies. In this game, you and your child will roll a game cube to determine how many pennies to either collect or give back to the pile. If you roll a 1, 3 or 4, you must collect that number of pennies. If you roll a 2 or 5, you must give back that many pennies to the pile. If you roll a 6, you can make a choice to either collect that many pennies or put that many pennies back. The player who gets exactly 5 pennies first wins. (The word *Pente* means "five." *Pentecost* means "fiftieth" in Greek.)

Prayer

As you tuck your little one into bed tonight, light your child's fire by reading the story of Pentecost while using a flashlight. Lead your child in this prayer: **Dear God, thank you for giving us your Holy Spirit. Thank you for always being with us. We love you. In Jesus' name, amen.**

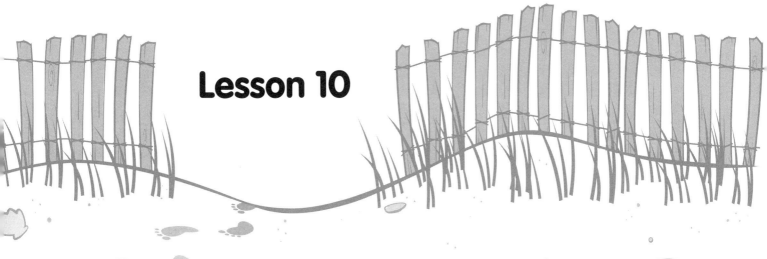

Lesson 10

DO YOU HEAR WHAT I HEAR?

Bible Story: 1 Kings 19:1–18
Bible Truth: God cares for us.
Bible Verse: I will listen to what God the LORD will say.
(Psalm 85:8)

Yelling, screaming, laughing and some tears—classrooms of younger children tend to be busy, active and noisy places. Draw attention to the quiet, still voice of the Lord God as you teach the story of Elijah. See if your children can hear what Elijah heard.

⬤ In this lesson children will **hear** the story of how Elijah listened to God.

⬤ In this lesson children will **learn** that God cared for Elijah and spoke to him in a whisper.

⬤ In this lesson children will **remember** that God cares for them.

LESSON TEN SNAPSHOT

Flippers Up
Reproducible Page

- [ ] Copies of page 81 for each child
- [x] Crayons or markers
- [ ] Scissors
- [ ] Glue
- [ ] Cotton balls
- [ ] Yarn

Splash-n-Spray

Bible Story Link:
Touched by an Angel
- [ ] Large piece of butcher paper
- [ ] Marker

Game:
What Did You Hear?
- [ ] Streamers

Extension Activity:
Dancing with Elijah
- [ ] CD, CD player

Soak It In
Bible Story Hands-on Activities

Activity 1:
An Angelic Snack
- [ ] Bread (one slice per child)
- [ ] Sugar and cinnamon mixture
- [ ] Butter
- [ ] Bowl
- [ ] Spoon
- [ ] Water
- [ ] Jar
- [ ] Craft sticks
- [ ] Cups (one per child)
- [ ] Paper plates (one per child)
- [ ] Angel-shaped cookie cutter

Activity 2:
Running to God
- [ ] Sticky notes
- [ ] Markers

Activity 3:
Cave Noises
- [ ] Table
- [ ] Blanket
- [ ] Empty paper towel rolls

Bible Story Time
- [ ] Bible
- [ ] Completed *Flippers Up* made from the reproducible page

Sail Away

Prayer
- [ ] None

Cleanup
- [ ] Brooms

Homeward Bound
- [ ] Completed *Flippers Up*
- [ ] Copy of *Home Connection* from page 86 for each child

HEART OF THE STORY

Elijah had just experienced one of the most amazing displays of God's power when he challenged the prophets of Baal. Now he was in despair, feeling lonely and depressed. Where was God during Elijah's emotional and spiritual turmoil? When God spoke to Elijah, he didn't appear in a display of power like he had in the past. God made himself known in the quietness of a still, small voice—a whisper. God works and reveals himself in truly mysterious ways, and typically how we least expect him to. Teach the children to stop and listen as you tell the story of how God loved and cared for Elijah.

Flippers Up
Bible Story Reproducible Page

Get List:
- A copy of the reproducible on this page for each child (you may want to copy onto tag board)
- Crayons or markers
- Scissors
- Glue
- Cotton balls
- Yarn

Have the children color and cut out the Elijah mask. Cut out the eyes. Have them glue cotton balls onto the reproducible for Elijah's beard and mustache. Glue pieces of yarn for Elijah's hair.

God cared for Elijah.
God cares for me.

Splash-n-Spray

Use these *Splash-n-Spray* activities to build knowledge that enriches the children's experience with the lesson while having fun.

Get List:
- Large piece of butcher paper
- Marker

Bible Story Link

Touched by an Angel
Lay the paper on the floor. Choose one child to lie on the piece of paper. Trace around the child's body to make an angel. Tell the children they will learn about an angel that took care of a man named Elijah. Have the children tell you the names of people who care for them. Write the names inside the angel figure. Ask them who cares for them more than anyone else. Fold the paper in half to represent the Bible. Give the children a clue. Tell them we learn about who loves and cares for us the most in the Bible. See if they can guess that it is God.

Get List:
- Streamers

Game

What Did You Hear?
Give each child a three-foot piece of streamer. Have the children line up on one side of the room with streamers in their hands. Tell the children they're going to pretend to be a man named Elijah. Elijah was listening for God to speak to him. When you say, **What did you hear?,** choose one child to reply, "wind," "earthquake," "fire" or "a whisper." If the answer is "wind," the child runs to the other side of the room flapping the streamer in the air and making wind noises. For "earthquake," the child makes a rumbling noise and waves the streamer on the floor while moving to other side of the room. For "fire," the child jumps to the other side of the room, waving the streamer up and down. For "whisper," the child silently walks to the other side of the room with the streamers hanging still. Continue going back and forth across the room until everyone has had a turn.

Get List:
- CD, CD player

Extension Activity

Dancing with Elijah
Assign certain children to be the earthquake, the wind, or the fire. Start the music and let the children dance as an earthquake, wind or fire moves. Stop the music. The children should stop dancing when the music stops. In your best whisper voice instruct the children to move a certain way (hop, skip, jump, wiggle, kneel in prayer, etc.). Turn the music back on and repeat. Let the children change "elements" if they want.

Soak It In
Bible Story Hands-on Activities

These activities can be used with large or small groups or as individual stations.

Get List:
- Bread (one slice per child)
- Sugar and cinnamon mixture
- Butter
- Bowl
- Spoon
- Water
- Jar
- Craft sticks
- Paper plates (one per child)
- Cups (one per child)
- Angel-shaped cookie cutter

Activity 1

An Angelic Snack

Distribute a paper plate, cup and one slice of bread to each child. Mix the cinnamon and sugar in a bowl. Use an angel-shaped cookie cutter to cut the bread. Have the children spread the angel with butter using the craft stick as a knife. Top off the butter with some sugar and cinnamon. Put water in a jar and have the children pass the jar and pour water into their cups. **Today we'll learn how an angel brought a snack of bread and water to Elijah.** *Note: Check with parents for any food allergies.*

Get List:
- Sticky notes
- Markers

Activity 2

Running to God

I will listen to what God the LORD will say. (Psalm 85:8)
Each child needs two sticky notes, one for the left shoe and one for the right shoe. The sticky notes for the left shoe should read: "I will listen." Those for the right shoe should read: "to what God the LORD will say." Attach sticky notes to the tops of shoes so children can read them. As the children walk around the room, they must say each phrase with each step. Practice with all the children stepping and saying the phrases together. Then see how fast they can say them. Discuss that Elijah was running for his life in the Bible story.

Get List:
- Table
- Blanket
- Empty paper towel rolls

Activity 3

Cave Noises

Have the children put a blanket over a table to make a cave. Tell them Elijah waited in a cave to hear from the Lord. As they play inside the cave, they can use the empty paper towel rolls to make different noises. Or you can use the towel rolls to make noises and have them guess the noises that are being made.

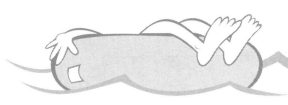

Soak It In
Bible Story Time

Get List:

- Bible
- Completed *Flippers Up* made from the reproducible page

Gather the children for story time. Be sure they have their *Flippers Up* ready to go. Hold up a Bible for the children to see. **In the Bible in the book of 1 Kings, there's a story about a man named Elijah.** Have children hold up their Elijah masks. Oh, there you are Elijah! Whenever I point to you, hold up your masks and say, "Where, oh where, has the good Lord gone? Where, oh where, can he be?"

Elijah was scared for his life. Queen Jezebel was going to kill him. Elijah had just proved that the Lord God was better than her gods. She was a wicked queen who was very mad at Elijah. So Elijah decided to run away (point).

Elijah ran for miles into the desert. Why wasn't God protecting him from the evil Queen Jezebel? The evil queen had killed many of God's people. Elijah felt lonely and far away from God. He sat down under a broom tree and wondered where God was. Elijah needed to hear from God (point).

Elijah was so sad and tired he fell asleep. He woke up when an angel touched him. The angel told Elijah to get up and eat. The angel gave him a cake of bread and a jar of water. Elijah ate the bread and drank the water. Elijah still wanted to hear from God (point).

Elijah fell asleep. Again the angel woke him up and told him to eat and drink. Elijah did eat and drink. He felt a little better, so he got up and started walking. He walked, and walked and walked for 40 days and 40 nights. Then he went to hide in a cave. Elijah still needed to hear from God (point).

What do you think Elijah heard when he was in the cave? Elijah heard the wind. The wind howled, and ripped, and roared and crashed. The mountain shuddered. The rocks split open, but the Lord was not in the wind (point).

After the wind came, Elijah was still sitting in the cave. All of a sudden, Elijah felt and heard an earthquake. The mountain heaved, and rolled and rumbled. But God was not in the earthquake (point).

After the earthquake, Elijah was still sitting in the cave. Suddenly, Elijah heard the snapping of flames from a huge fire. Flames leaped up all around him. But the Lord was not in the fire (point).

After the wind, the earthquake and the great fire, Elijah sat in the stillness of the cave. All of a sudden, he heard a gentle whisper. It was God. God cared for Elijah. God told Elijah he was not alone (point). **God was with Elijah. God is with us too.**

- Why did Elijah feel lonely? *(because Queen Jezebel was after him)*
- Why did Elijah want to hear from God? *(he was afraid and didn't know what to do)*
- How did God finally let Elijah know he was with him? *(in a gentle whisper)*

Sail Away

Get List:
- None

Prayer

Ask the children to tell you how a big wind sounds. Have them tell you how an earthquake sounds. Then have them tell you how a great fire sounds. Now have the children tell you how it sounded when God whispered to Elijah. Have them whisper to you things they remember from the Bible story. Then lead the children in this prayer: **Dear God, thank you for always being with us. Help me to know that you are always near, and help me hear your voice. Thank you for always loving and caring for us. In Jesus' name, amen.**

Get List:
- Brooms

Cleanup

Have the children use brooms to clean up. They can sweep up the toys or put them on the brooms as they carry them to where they belong. Talk about how Elijah sat under a broom tree while he was in the desert.

Get List:
- Completed *Flippers Up*
- Copy of *Home Connection* for each child

Homeward Bound

As the children leave, make sure they have their completed *Flippers Up* they made for Bible Story Time. Have the children put on their Elijah masks. Tell them their masks remind you of Elijah. Elijah learned that God loves and cares for us. Elijah heard God talk to him in a whisper voice.

- Why did Elijah run into the desert and hide in a cave?
- Who was always with Elijah even though he felt lonely?

PINT-SIZE BIBLE BITES

When Elijah ran from Jezebel into the desert and to Mount Horeb, he covered 200 miles on foot.

TEACHER TIP

If some children don't want to use the Elijah mask or participate in other ways, don't make an issue out of it. Instead, focus on the children who are participating. This will typically evoke a change of heart in the non-participants, as they want to be praised for positive behavior also.

Home Connection
Dive In!

Title: Do You Hear What I Hear?

Bible Story: 1 Kings 19:1-18

Bible Truth: God cares for us.

Bible Verse: I will listen to what God the LORD will say. (Psalm 85:8)

- In this lesson your child **heard** the story of how Elijah listened to God.

- In this lesson your child **learned** that God cared for Elijah and spoke to him in a whisper.

- In this lesson your child **remembered** that God cares for him or her.

In this Bible story, Elijah was running from Queen Jezebel, who wanted to kill him. He was one of the last remaining prophets of God, because she had already killed many of the others. Elijah was exhausted and feeling defeated. He ran to the desert and finally to the mountains. It was there he waited for God to speak to him. He heard a mighty wind, an earthquake and a fierce fire. But God wasn't in those. Then he heard God speaking to him in a whisper. God can present himself to us in spectacular ways or in simple ways. Remind your children that either way, God is always with them.

HOME CONNECTIONS

These are items used during the Bible story lesson that might be commonly found in your home. When your child sees or plays with one of the items mentioned below, help make the connection to the Bible story.

Bread: The children made bread angels. When you eat bread, remind your child that in the Bible story, an angel visited Elijah twice while he was in the desert. The angel brought him bread and water to eat because God cared for Elijah just like God cares for your little one.

Broom: A broom was used to help clean up. When you use a broom, remind your child of the broom tree that Elijah sat under while he was in the desert. If possible, find a picture of a broom tree to show your child.

KEEPING CONNECTED

Here are two simple activities that were used in class during the Bible story lesson, Do You Hear

What I Hear? Use these activities to help your child remember the Bible story lesson.

Cave Noises

Build a cave in your home. Drape a blanket over a table to make the cave. Talk about how Elijah waited in a cave to hear from the Lord. As your child plays inside the cave, use an empty paper towel roll to make different noises. See if your child can guess the noises that are being made.

What Did You Hear?

Give your child a three-foot piece of streamer. In our story, Elijah was listening for God to speak to him. Ask your child, **What did you hear?** Choose either "wind," "earthquake," "fire" or "a whisper." If you say wind, have your child run while flapping the streamer in the air and making wind noises. If you call out earthquake, have your child make a rumble noise while waving the streamer on the floor. If you call out fire, have your child jump while waving the streamer up and down. Then if you call out whisper, have your child walk silently while holding the streamer still.

Prayer

As you tuck your child into bed tonight, use a whisper voice. Use the whisper voice to read a book or read a Bible story. Then use a whisper voice as you pray: **Dear God, thank you for loving and caring for _____ (child's name). Help him/her to always listen to you. Help _____ to always know that you are with him/her. In Jesus' name, amen.**

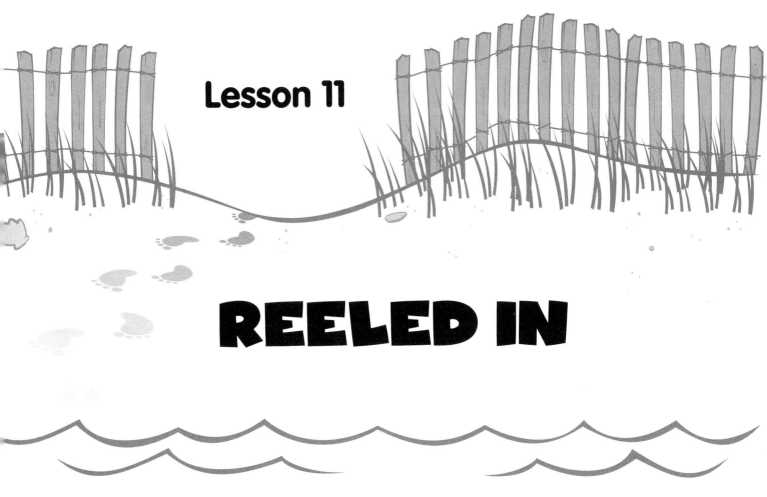

Lesson 11

REELED IN

Bible Story: Matthew 4:18–22

Bible Truth: Jesus wants us to follow him.

Bible Verse: "Come, follow me," Jesus said, "and I will make you fishers of men." (Mark 1:17)

Children usually follow anyone who is willing to lead them. Have fun as you reel them in and introduce them to Jesus. Teach them to follow Jesus and know that they can always trust him.

◉ In this lesson children will **hear** the story of how Jesus called his disciples to be fishers of men.

◉ In this lesson children will **learn** that Jesus wants us to follow him.

◉ In this lesson children will **remember** to follow Jesus.

LESSON ELEVEN SNAPSHOT

Flippers Up
Reproducible Page

- ☐ Copies of page 89 for each child
- ☑ Scissors
- ☐ Crayons or markers
- ☐ Tape

Splash-n-Spray

Bible Story Link:
Follow Me
- ☐ Several beach towels

Game:
Drop Your Nets
- ☐ Several beach towels

Extension Activity:
Follow Your Leader Magnets
- ☐ Cardstock
- ☐ Assorted fish stickers
- ☐ Stick-on magnets

Soak It In
Bible Story Hands-on Activities

Activity 1:
Fishy Men
- ☐ Paper plates or paper towels
- ☐ Fish-shaped crackers
- ☐ Paper
- ☐ Markers

Activity 2:
Fishing for Men
- ☐ 24 index cards
- ☐ 24 paper clips
- ☐ Yarn or string
- ☐ Tape
- ☐ Markers
- ☐ Straws
- ☐ Magnets

Activity 3:
Sand Art
- ☐ White construction paper
- ☐ Marker
- ☐ Craft glue
- ☐ Bowls
- ☐ 3 different colors of gelatin
- ☐ Spoons
- ☐ Paintbrushes or cotton swabs or craft sticks

Bible Story Time
- ☐ Bible
- ☐ Completed *Flippers Up* made from the reproducible page including pictures

Sail Away

Prayer
- ☐ Long rope

Cleanup
- ☐ None

Homeward Bound
- ☐ Completed *Flippers Up*
- ☐ Copy of *Home Connection* from page 94 for each child
- ☐ Paper
- ☐ Marker
- ☐ Scissors

HEART OF THE STORY

In this Bible story Jesus asks the disciples to drop everything and follow him. Their response was immediate. They did not consult with others. They did not check their bank accounts to see if they could swing it. They did not have a back-up plan. All of their skills were wrapped up in the only job they had done their whole lives—fish. When Jesus calls us, he equips us with everything we need. He will help us through the journey, even when we go through some rough waters. Teach your children that all they truly need in life is to follow Jesus. Get them reeled in!

Flippers Up
Bible Story Reproducible Page

Get List:
- A copy of the reproducible on this page for each child
- Scissors
- Crayons or markers
- Tape

Have the children color the small pictures and story board. Tell the children you'll collect the small pictures so they might not get back the ones they color. Children cut on all solid lines. You might cut out the two narrow rectangular slits. Collect the numbered pictures and sort them by number. Children fold on the broken lines and tape as shown to make their story boards.

CUT OUT

Follow me!

FOLD

"Come, follow me," Jesus said, "and I will make you fishers of men." Mark 1:17

CUT OUT

TAPE

TAPE

Splash-n-Spray

Use these *Splash-n-Spray* activities to build knowledge that enriches the children's experience with the lesson while having fun.

Get List:
- Several beach towels

Bible Story Link

Follow Me
Make a path with beach towels. The path can be straight or in a circle. Spread the towels out far enough so the children must jump a little to get from one to the next. Have all the children line up behind you, then have them follow you. As they follow, perform an action they must do as well. For example, hop, clap or snap. Have the children take turns being the leader. Talk about how Jesus was a leader and wants us to follow him.

Get List:
- Several beach towels

Game

Drop Your Nets
Give each pair or group of two to four children a beach towel. Have all the groups start at one end of the room. Each player in a group grabs a corner of the towel. Groups must get to the other side of the room. Select one person to tag others. If the group is tagged they must go back to the starting line. If a group drops their net (beach towel), they are safe from being tagged. Groups cannot advance forward until they pick up their nets and continue. Discuss how Jesus asked the disciples to drop their nets and follow him—and they did.

Get List:
- Cardstock
- Assorted fish stickers
- Stick-on magnets

Extension Activity

Follow Your Leader Magnets
Cut the cardstock into three-inch squares. Write the Bible Verse "Come, follow me," Jesus said, "and I will make you fishers of men." (Mark 1:17) on the cardstock. Have children add stickers to the squares. Stick the magnet onto the back of the squares. Tell the kids they can put this fish magnet on their refrigerator to remind them to tell others about Jesus.

Soak It In
Bible Story Hands-on Activities

These activities can be used with large or small groups or as individual stations.

Get List:
- Paper plates or paper towels
- Fish-shaped crackers
- Paper
- Markers

Activity 1

Fishy Men

Give each child a plate or paper towel and a handful of crackers. Have them use the fish crackers to make the shape of a man. You might want to draw the basic shape of a person as an example. Discuss how the disciples were fishermen, and Jesus turned them into fishers of men. *Note: Check with parents for any food allergies.*

Get List:
- 24 index cards
- 24 paper clips
- Yarn or string
- Tape
- Markers
- Straws
- Magnets

Activity 2

Fishing for Men

"Come, follow me," Jesus said, "and I will make you fishers of men." (Mark 1:17)

Make several fishing poles by taping string to a straw and attaching a magnet at the other end of the string. Cut 14 index cards into the shape of a man. On each card, write one of the words from the Bible Verse, including the reference. Cut 10 index cards into fish shapes. Attach a small paper clip to each figure. Place all the figures in a pile. Have the children try to fish out only the men using the poles. Once all the men have been fished out, have the children put the Bible Verse together.

Get List:
- White construction paper
- Marker
- Craft glue
- Bowls
- 3 different colors of gelatin
- Spoons
- Paintbrushes or cotton swabs or craft sticks

Activity 3

Sand Art

Draw fish and men on white construction paper. Empty gelatin into bowls, and put spoons in each bowl. Have the children use paintbrushes, cotton swabs or craft sticks to spread a thin layer of glue to cover the fish and men on their papers. Then help them sprinkle gelatin onto the glue. Tap off any excess gelatin back into the bowls. Talk about how their pictures remind you of a sandy beach. Jesus was on a beach when he called his disciples to follow him.

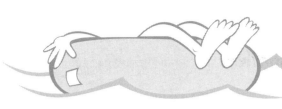

Soak It In
Bible Story Time

Get List:
- Bible
- Completed *Flippers Up* made from the reproducible page
- Pictures

Gather the children for story time. Be sure they have their *Flippers Up* ready to go. Hold up a Bible for the children to see. **In the Bible in the book of Matthew, we learn how Jesus chose his disciples. Disciples are the men who followed Jesus.**

One day Jesus was walking along the beach. He saw two men, Peter and his brother Andrew, out in their boat fishing. Jesus watched as they threw their nets into the water. When they pulled their nets in, they were full of fish. Peter and Andrew were good at fishing. **Do you see the two men fishing on your *Flippers Up*? Let's help them catch some fish.** Toss out all the fish pictures labeled 1 from the *Flippers Up* page. Have each child gather one fish and put it in the fishing net.

Jesus had been watching Peter and Andrew while they were fishing. Jesus wanted these two brothers to join him to help him tell others about God. Jesus also wanted them to learn how to fish for men instead of fish. When Jesus asked Peter and Andrew to join him in fishing for men, do you know what they said? They said yes. Both men left their fishing nets and followed Jesus. **Turn your *Flippers Up* to the other side. Let's help Peter and Andrew fish for men.** Toss out all the pictures of men labeled 2. Have each child gather one man and tuck it in next to the men on their *Flippers Up*.

Jesus started to walk down the beach again. This time he saw two other fishermen preparing their nets and getting ready to go fishing. The two men were James and John. They were also brothers and they both loved to fish. **Turn your *Flippers Up* to find the two men with their nets. Let's help them catch some fish.** Toss out all the fish labeled 3. Have each child gather one fish and tuck it in the fishing net.

Jesus called out to James and John. Jesus wanted them to follow him. Jesus wanted James and John to help him teach others about God. Jesus asked James and John to join him and fish for men. Do you know what James and John did? They left their nets and followed Jesus. James and John decided to help Jesus fish for men. **Turn your *Flippers Up*. Let's help James and John fish for men.** Toss out all the men labeled 4. Have each child gather one man and tuck it next to the other men on their *Flippers Up*.

Now Jesus has found four helpers: Peter, Andrew, James and John. These four men became Jesus' disciples. These men would follow Jesus for a long time. They would learn about Jesus and about God. They would help Jesus tell others about God. They were now fishers of men.

- **Why did Peter, Andrew, James and John drop their fishing nets?** *(Jesus asked them to follow him.)*
- **What does it mean to fish for men?** *(to tell others about God)*
- **Why did Jesus want Peter, Andrew, James and John to fish for men?** *(he needed people to help him)*

Sail Away

Get List:
- Long rope

Prayer

Gather the children. Say, **I'm going fishing for men**. Throw the rope to a child, and tell him or her to hang on to one end. Then reel in that child. Ask that child to tell you one thing he or she remembers from the Bible story. Repeat until all the children have had a turn. Then close with this prayer: **Dear God, help us to be fishers of men. Help us to tell others about you. In Jesus' name, amen.**

Get List:
- None

Cleanup

As the children clean up, have them swim like fish to pick up their toys. Then have them walk like a "man" when they go to put the toys back where they belong. You can sing the song, "I will make you fishers of men" while the children clean if desired.

Get List:
- Completed *Flippers Up*
- Copy of *Home Connection* for each child
- Paper
- Marker
- Scissors

Homeward Bound

As the children leave, make sure they have their completed *Flippers Up* they made for Bible Story Time. Cut a piece of paper into 2 x 3-inch rectangles. Write a U on each rectangle, and give one to each child. Tell the child, **The U reminds me of you! U can be fishers of men, too. U can follow Jesus. U can tell others about Jesus.** Have the children tuck their U's into their *Flippers Up*.

- How can you follow Jesus?
- Who wants us to follow him?

PINT-SIZE BIBLE BITES

In 1986 a fishing boat was found in an archeological dig off the shore of the Sea of Galilee, and was thought to be around 2,000 years old. Subsequently, it was named "The Jesus Boat."

TEACHER TIP

When teaching lessons that require the children to move about, then return to their seats, it's helpful to have assigned spots or rows. These are easily made with masking tape or electrical tape. Electrical tape comes in colors and doesn't leave a sticky residue on the carpet when removed.

Home Connection
Dive In!

Title: Reeled In

Bible Story: Matthew 4:18–22

Bible Truth: Jesus wants us to follow him.

Bible Verse: "Come, follow me," Jesus said, "and I will make you fishers of men." (Mark 1:17)

⬤ In this lesson your child **heard** the story of how Jesus called his disciples to be fishers of men.

⬤ In this lesson your child **learned** that Jesus wants us to follow him.

⬤ In this lesson your child **remembered** to follow Jesus.

In this Bible story, Jesus was walking along a beach. He saw Peter and Andrew out fishing in their boat. He called them to leave their nets and become fishers of men. Shortly after, Jesus called out to James and John, who were also fishermen preparing their nets along the shore. These four men became Jesus' first disciples. They dropped everything they had to follow Jesus. Reel in your children by teaching them to follow Jesus.

HOME CONNECTIONS

This item was used during the Bible story lesson. When your child sees or plays with this item mentioned below, help make the connection to the Bible story.

Fish: Fish crackers, fishing poles and fishing nets were used and discussed during this Bible story. If you have an opportunity, take your child fishing. Talk about how the men in the Bible story were fishermen. Discuss how they stopped fishing to follow Jesus.

KEEPING CONNECTED

Here are two simple activities that were used in class during the Bible story lesson, Reeled In. Use these activities to help your child remember the Bible story lesson.

Follow Me

Make a path using beach towels. The path can be straight or in a circle. Spread towels out far enough so your child must jump a little to get from one to the next. Have your child follow you while you perform an action that your child must do as well. For example: hop, clap or snap. Discuss how Jesus was a leader and wants us to follow him. Have your child be the leader and you follow.

Sand Art

Cut out fish or men shapes from white paper. Empty different colors of gelatin into bowls, and put spoons in each. Use paintbrushes, cotton swabs or craft sticks to paint glue onto the fish or men shapes. Help your child sprinkle gelatin onto the glue. Tap off any excess gelatin back into the bowls. Talk about how the picture reminds you of a sandy beach. Jesus was on a beach when he called for his disciples to follow him.

Prayer

Draw a U with your finger on your child's back before tucking him or her into bed. See if your child can guess what the letter is. Each time you say U, draw it again on your child's back. Talk about all the things your child or you can do. Then talk about how you can follow Jesus. Lead your child in this prayer: **Dear God, thank U for _____(your child's name). Help us to follow U and love U. In Jesus' name, amen.**

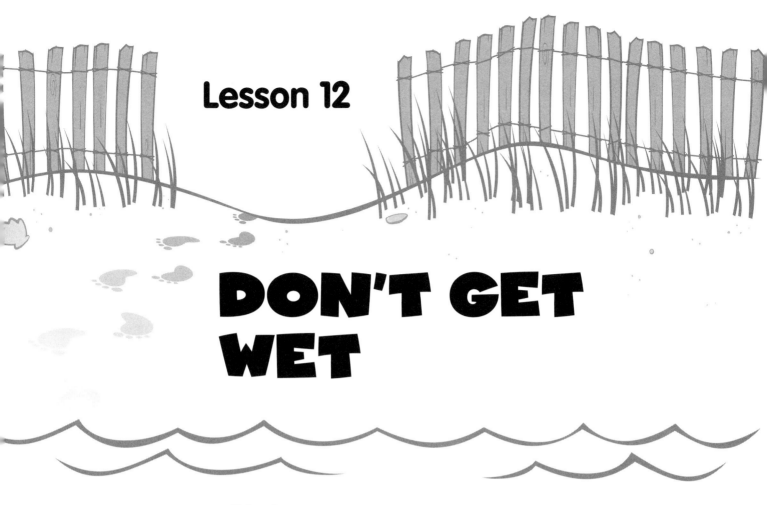

Lesson 12

DON'T GET WET

Bible Story: Matthew 14:22–33

Bible Truth: Jesus is the Son of God.

Bible Verse: Let us fix our eyes on Jesus, the author and perfecter of our faith. (Hebrews 12:2)

Lightning, thunder, wind and rain—storms can be pretty terrifying events for children. Life is full of scary trials. But God does not want us to be afraid. Teach your children that when scary feelings come, they can keep their eyes fixed on Jesus. They can trust the Son of God to help them weather the storms of life.

- In this lesson children will **hear** the story of how Jesus walked on the water.

- In this lesson children will **learn** that Jesus is God's Son.

- In this lesson children will **remember** to keep their eyes on Jesus because they can trust him.

LESSON TWELVE SNAPSHOT

Flippers Up
Reproducible Page

- [ ] Copy of the reproducible on page 97 for each child
- [ ] Markers or crayons
- [ ] Metal brads
- [ ] Straws
- [ ] Scissors
- [ ] Hole punch

Splash-n-Spray

Bible Story Link:
Family Ties
- [ ] Necktie
- [ ] Sticky notes
- [ ] Marker or pen

Game:
Name Game
- [ ] Index cards (two per child)
- [ ] Marker

Extension Activity:
Eyes on Jesus
- [ ] Toilet tissue tubes (two per child)
- [ ] Construction paper
- [ ] Tape
- [ ] Markers
- [ ] Optional: stickers

Soak It In
Bible Story
Hands-on Activities

Activity 1:
Don't Rock the Boat
- [ ] Paper plates
- [ ] Pear halves
- [ ] Teddy bear-shaped graham crackers
- [ ] Can of whipped cream
- [ ] Forks

Activity 2:
Eye Spy
- [ ] Chenille wires (two per child)
- [ ] Large sheet of paper
- [ ] Marker
- [ ] Scissors

Activity 3:
Sink or Float
- [ ] Tub of water
- [ ] Various items in your classroom
- [ ] Paper
- [ ] Markers

Bible Story Time
- [ ] Bible
- [ ] Completed *Flippers Up* made from the reproducible page

Sail Away

Prayer
- [ ] Completed *Flippers Up*

Cleanup
- [ ] A picture of Jesus
- [ ] A picture of Jesus on a large sun

Homeward Bound
- [ ] Completed *Flippers Up*
- [ ] Copy of *Home Connection* from page 102 for each child

HEART OF THE STORY

Can you imagine Jesus reaching out his hand to you and you placing your hand in his? Life has a way of producing a lot of wind and horrific waves. Anytime you feel yourself sinking into the quagmire of life, close your eyes and picture Jesus reaching his hand out to you. Toss your little ones a life preserver as you teach them about Jesus, God's Son, in this lesson. He is the one we can always trust to keep us from sinking!

Flippers Up
Bible Story Reproducible Page

Get List:
- A copy of this page for each child
- Markers or crayons
- Metal brads
- Straws
- Scissors

Cut a one-inch piece of straw for each child. Have the children color the circles, then cut them out. On circle A, cut the solid lines and fold up on the broken lines. Punch the center holes on A and B. Insert the brad through A, the straw, then B. Show the children how to blow to spin A showing J-E-S-U-S and the wind and the waves.

Splash-n-Spray

Use these *Splash-n-Spray* activities to build knowledge that enriches the children's experience with the lesson while having fun.

Get List:
- Necktie
- Sticky notes
- Marker or pen

Bible Story Link

Family Ties
Put a necktie around your neck that has sticky notes attached that identify the names and relation of your family members. Include sticky notes for God, Jesus' Father, and Jesus, God's Son. Beginning with the notes of your family relations, remove and read each sticky note. Explain how each person is related to you. Last, remove the sticky notes for God and Jesus. Explain how they are related to each other, emphasizing that Jesus is God's Son.

Get List:
- Index cards (two per child)
- Marker

Game

Name Game
Write each child's first name on a card and last name on another card. Have the children sit in a circle. Mix the cards, names down, in the center of the circle. Have the children turn over cards to find the ones with their names. Talk about how we all have different names and most of us have a first, middle and last name. But we also called by other names such as son, daughter, grandchild, etc. and we call others by different names such as dad, mom, aunt, cousin, and so on.

Get List:
- Toilet tissue tubes (2 per child)
- Construction paper
- Tape
- Markers
- Optional: stickers

Extension Activity

Eyes on Jesus
Fold construction paper to be as wide as toilet tissue tubes are long. Wrap the paper around two tubes and use tape to construct binoculars. Let the children decorate their binoculars with markers or stickers. Look through the binoculars, pretending to see Jesus coming. React as the disciples might have. Remind the children to keep their eyes on Jesus because they can trust him.

Soak It In
Bible Story Hands-on Activities

These activities can be used with large or small groups or as individual stations.

Get List:
- Paper plates
- Pear halves
- Bear-shaped graham crackers
- Can of whipped cream
- Forks

Don't Rock the Boat

Direct the children to put a pear half "boat" on their paper plates. Then stand bear-cracker sailors and passengers in the fruit. Spread whipped cream on the plate around the boat for water. Set sail and enjoy as you explain today's lesson is about the disciples in a boat. *Note: Check with parents for any food allergies.*

Get List:
- Chenille wires (two per child)
- Large sheet of paper
- Marker
- Scissors

Eye Spy

Let us fix our eyes on Jesus, the author and perfecter of our faith. (Hebrews 12:2)

Write the Bible Verse on a large piece of paper. Give each child two chenille wires. Bend one wire in half, looping each end to the middle and wrap to connect making the two eye lenses of glasses. Cut the other wire in half and attach these to the lenses, creating the ear pieces. Curve the ends to wrap around the ears. Have everyone put on their glasses to see your verse poster. Point to each word as you say the Bible Verse together. Say a word from the verse and have a child point to it.

Get List:
- Tub of water
- Various items in your classroom
- Paper
- Markers

Sink or Float

Put out a tub of water and a paper marked "Sinkers" and a paper marked "Floaters". Read each sign aloud to help the children read them too. Let the children test items in your room to determine which ones sink and which ones float in a tub of water. Have them sort the items as either "sinkers" or "floaters." Ask if they think they would sink or float if they stepped onto the water. Talk about how they will learn an amazing thing that happened in the Bible story—Jesus and Peter both walked on water. As an extension, show the children how to make a picture graph identifying the items that sink and the ones that float.

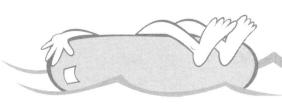

Soak It In
Bible Story Time

Get List:
- Bible
- Completed *Flippers Up* made from the reproducible on page 97

Gather the children for story time. Be sure they have their *Flippers Up* ready to go. **To help me with this Bible story, you're going to supply wind and waves. When I say "the wind," turn your *Flippers Up* to show me the pictures of the wind and waves and say, "the wind was blowing; the waves were growing."**

Hold up a Bible for the children to see. **The Bible tell us, in the book of Matthew, about a time when Jesus told his disciples to get into a boat and sail to the other side of a lake. Jesus wanted some time to be alone to pray. So Jesus went up the mountainside by himself to find a quiet place to pray. While he prayed the disciples sailed out on the lake in the boat. But while they were in the boat, <u>the</u> <u>wind</u> …**

The disciples were fishermen, and they were used to being in a boat. They were working hard to row the boat against <u>the</u> <u>wind</u> … Suddenly they saw someone walking on the water coming right toward them. They were all afraid. They thought it was a ghost. It was hard to see because <u>the</u> <u>wind</u> …

It was Jesus walking on the water. He was done praying and walked out on the water to join the disciples. He knew they were afraid so He said, "Be brave. It is I. Don't be afraid." Peter wanted to be sure it was really Jesus so he said, "If it's really you, tell me to come to you on the water."

Jesus said, "Come."

Peter got out of the boat and walked on the water toward Jesus. Peter looked at Jesus and walked on top of the water. But then he looked away at <u>the</u> <u>wind</u>.

When Peter stopped paying attention to Jesus and looked away is when Peter began to sink. Peter yelled for help. Immediately Jesus reached out and grabbed Peter.

As Jesus and Peter climbed into the boat, the rest of the disciples bowed down and worshipped Jesus because they realized that he is the Son of God.

The disciples learned that no matter what is going on around us, we can always trust Jesus. Just keep your eyes on him.

- **Who can we always trust?** *(Jesus)*
- **Who is the Son of God?** *(Jesus)*
- **Why should we keep our eyes on Jesus?** *(because he is the Son of God)*

Sail Away

Get List:
- Completed *Flippers Up*

Prayer

Have the children turn their *Flippers Up* windmills to see the wind and waves. Explain that Peter took his eyes off of Jesus because the wind and the waves distracted him. It is similar for us; it just might not be the wind and waves that distracts us from thinking about Jesus. Have the children turn their windmills back to see the name of Jesus. Lead them in this prayer: **Dear God, thank you for Jesus. Help us keep our eyes on Jesus. Help us trust him in all that we do. In Jesus' name, amen.**

Get List:
- A picture of Jesus
- A picture of Jesus on a large sun

Cleanup

As the children clean up, pretend a big storm blows in. Have the children pretend they are in the storm. Use a picture of Jesus to have them keep their eyes on him as they continue to clean up. Bring out a picture of the sun, and pretend the day is very nice. Keep changing the weather, but have the kids keep their eyes on Jesus.

Get List:
- Completed *Flippers Up*
- Copy of *Home Connection* for each child

Homeward Bound

As the children leave, make sure they have their completed *Flippers Up* and a *Home Connection*. Have the children put on their eye-spy glasses. Tell them their eye-spy glasses can remind them to keep their eyes on Jesus.

- Who can trust Jesus?
- Who is the Son of God?

PINT-SIZE BIBLE BITES

The miraculous events had a good and powerful effect on the disciples, prompting them to worship Jesus and declare the truth about him.

TEACHER TIP

Discuss with your children how following your instructions and obeying the rules of the classroom are ways they can keep their eyes on Jesus. If you have children that do not follow the rules, it may be necessary to take away their privilege of playing at a particular activity center.

Home Connection
Dive In!

Title: Don't Get Wet

Bible Story: Matthew 14:22–33

Bible Truth: Jesus is the Son of God.

Bible Verse: Let us fix our eyes on Jesus, the author and perfecter of our faith. (Hebrews 12:2)

- In this lesson your child **heard** the story of how Jesus walked on the water.
- In this lesson your child **learned** that Jesus is God's Son.
- In this lesson your child **remembered** to keep his or her eyes on Jesus because they can trust him.

The disciples were in the boat when Jesus walked toward them on the water. The disciples were terrified; they thought it was a ghost. Jesus called out to them and Peter responded. Peter stepped out of the boat and walked on the water toward him. Once Peter looked at the waves and took his eyes off Jesus, he began to sink. Jesus reached out to Peter, and the two of them returned to the boat. The disciples were amazed by what they saw. They realized Jesus truly is the Son of God. When you or your child begin to sink due to the winds and waves of life, be sure to reach for Jesus' hand.

HOME CONNECTIONS

These are items used during the Bible story lesson that might be commonly found in your home. When your child sees or plays with one of the items mentioned below, help make the connection to the Bible story.

Boats: This Bible story takes place in a boat. The next time your child is in the bathtub, grab a toy boat and retell the Bible story.

Eyeglasses: Eyeglasses were used as a reminder to keep our eyes on Jesus. When your child gets scared, you might want to get a pair of eyeglasses as a reminder that we can look to Jesus when we're afraid.

KEEPING CONNECTED

Here are two simple activities that were used in class during the Bible story lesson, Don't Get Wet. Use these activities to help your child remember the Bible story lesson.

Don't Rock the Boat

Make boats using half a pear. Add bear-shaped graham crackers for people, and use whipped cream for the water around the boat. Then eat while you talk about the Bible story. Discuss what the disciples learned, and especially Peter when he got out of the boat.

Family Ties

Put a necktie around your neck that has sticky notes attached that identify the names and relation of your family members. Include sticky notes for God, Jesus' Father, and Jesus, God's Son. Beginning with the notes of your family relations, remove and read each sticky note. Explain how each person is related and maybe find each in a photo album. Last, remove the sticky notes for God and Jesus. Explain how they are related to each other, emphasizing that Jesus is God's Son.

Prayer

It is so important that your child feels like a part of a family. Share pictures of family members and talk about them. Then pray this prayer together: **Dear God, thank you so much for our family. Help us to keep our eyes on you. We love you. In Jesus' name, amen.**

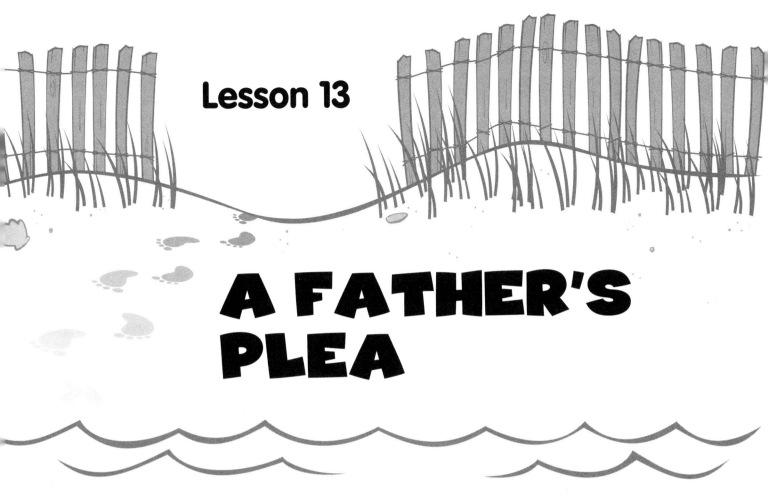

Lesson 13

A FATHER'S PLEA

Bible Story: Luke 8:40–42, 49–56

Bible Truth: Be thankful for all things.

Bible Verse: Devote yourselves to prayer, being watchful and thankful. (Colossians 4:2)

When children are in need, they typically call out to a parent. We want children to progressively learn to become dependent upon God and call out to him. In this Bible story, Jairus cries out to Jesus for help. Teach your children to cry out to Jesus both in times of need and in times of thanksgiving.

- In this lesson children will **hear** the story of Jairus and how Jesus healed his daughter.

- In this lesson children will **learn** that Jairus called out to Jesus when his daughter was sick and was thankful when she was well.

- In this lesson children will **remember** that we should have thankful hearts.

LESSON THIRTEEN SNAPSHOT

Flippers Up
Reproducible Page

- ☐ A copy of the reproducible on page 105 for each child
- ☐ Scissors
- ☐ Tape
- ☐ Markers or crayons

Splash-n-Spray

Bible Story Link:
Heart to Heart
- ☐ Large poster board
- ☐ Plastic bandages
- ☐ Permanent marker
- ☐ Tape

Game:
Hands of Thanks
- ☐ Chairs
- ☐ Paper
- ☐ Scissors

Extension Activity:
Thank You Letter
- ☐ Big paper (butcher paper)
- ☐ Washable markers

Soak It In
Bible Story
Hands-on Activities

Activity 1:
Full of Thanks
- ☐ Scoop-shaped corn chips
- ☐ Oat ring cereal
- ☐ Raisins
- ☐ Bowls

Activity 2:
Hands of Prayer
- ☐ Construction paper
- ☐ Markers
- ☐ Scissors
- ☐ Tape

Activity 3:
Hearts of Thanks
- ☐ Construction paper
- ☐ Tissue paper
- ☐ Scissors
- ☐ Marker
- ☐ Glue
- ☐ Pencils

Bible Story Time
- ☐ Bible
- ☐ Completed *Flippers Up* made from the reproducible page

Sail Away

Prayer
- ☐ Completed *Flippers Up*

Cleanup
- ☐ None

Homeward Bound
- ☐ Completed *Flippers Up*
- ☐ Construction paper hearts
- ☐ Copy of *Home Connection* from page 110 for each child

HEART OF THE STORY

Have you ever found yourself in a situation or dilemma that seems beyond help or hope? This is how Jairus felt when he discovered his daughter was dead. Jairus had faith that Jesus could do something about it. Jesus can do the impossible. He can heal the deepest wounds. He can mend the most broken relationships. If it seems as though there is no hope, Jesus can give you hope. Shine a ray of hope on your children as you tell them how Jesus reaches out his hand and heals us.

Flippers Up
Bible Story Reproducible Page

Get List:
- A copy of the reproducible on this page for each child
- Scissors
- Tape
- Markers or crayons

Have the children color the pictures. Cut out the large figure. Fold on the broken lines on the sides of the hearts and tape the tab on 1 to the back side of 3. Fold on the broken line on the top of the hearts to bring hearts to the inside.

Splash-n-Spray

Use these *Splash-n-Spray* activities to build knowledge that enriches the children's experience with the lesson while having fun.

Get List:
- Large poster board
- Plastic bandages
- Permanent marker
- Tape

Bible Story Link

Heart to Heart
Cut a large heart from poster board. Give each child a bandage. Ask the children to tell about a time when they've been hurt. Write that physical hurt on each one's bandage. Then have the children stick their bandages to the heart. Tape the heart on the wall. Talk about how Jesus can heal all our hurts.

Get List:
- Chairs
- Paper
- Scissors

Game

Hands of Thanks
Cut out several paper hearts. Place several chairs at opposite ends of the room. Put the hearts on one chair. The class must spread out, then try to get the hearts from one chair to another by passing the hearts from one player to another as they respond with, "Thanks." Allow every child several chances to pass a heart. Talk about how Jesus reached out his hand to a girl in the Bible story.

Get List:
- Big paper (butcher paper)
- Washable markers

Extension Activity

Thank You Letter
Begin a letter with "Dear God, Thank you for ..." and continue with the children's suggestions. Close with "Love." and then read the letter aloud. Let the children write their names and decorate the letter with pictures. Hang the letter on the wall.

Soak It In
Bible Story Hands-on Activities

These activities can be used with large or small groups or as individual stations.

Get List:
- Scoop-shaped corn chips
- Oat ring cereal
- Raisins
- Bowls

Activity 1

Full of Thanks
Put the raisins and oat ring cereal into bowls. Have the children use the scoop-shaped chips to scoop up thanks. As they scoop, have them say, "Thankful hearts are happy hearts." Tell them they'll learn about a family who had very thankful hearts. *Note: Check with parents for food allergies.*

Get List:
- Construction paper
- Markers
- Scissors
- Tape

Activity 2

Hands of Prayer
Devote yourselves to prayer, being watchful and thankful. (Colossians 4:2)

Have the children trace their hands onto construction paper, then cut them out. On each finger of each hand, help them write a word from the Bible memory verse, including the reference. The children can tape the hands together with the words facing out. Have them repeat the verse aloud several times using their hands of prayer.

Get List:
- Construction paper
- Tissue paper
- Scissors
- Marker
- Glue
- Pencils

Activity 3

Hearts of Thanks
Cut out large hearts from the construction paper. Cut the tissue paper into two-inch squares. Write T H A N K S in block letters on each child's paper heart. Have the children take a square of tissue paper. Stick the eraser end of a pencil in the center of a square. Wrap the tissue paper up and twist it around the pencil. Dip the end of the tissue paper in the glue and stick it on a letter. Continue gluing tissue paper until the letters of the word THANKS are covered.

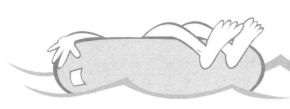

Soak It In
Bible Story Time

Get List:
- Bible
- Completed *Flippers Up* made from the reproducible page

Gather the children for story time. Be sure they have their *Flippers Up* ready to go. Before starting, make sure the children have all their hearts tucked in. Have the children look at the heart numbered 1 on their *Flippers Up*. **What do you see on heart number one?** *(some people)* **Yes, in fact there was a large crowd gathered. The people came to see Jesus. Find the man who is sad. His name is Jairus. The Bible tells us about Jairus.** Hold up a Bible for the children to see.

His daughter was very sick; so sick she was about to die. Jairus wanted to ask Jesus to come help. But that's not all. Have the children flip up the heart from the inside. **When you flip up the heart you can see, a heart full of thanksgiving. Jairus is thankful Jesus is there and that he could go to Jesus for help.**

Have the children look at heart number 2. **What do you see?** *(Jesus and Jairus)* **This is a picture of Jesus with Jairus. But do you see how sad they are? They are sad because they just received news that Jairus' daughter actually died.** Have the children flip up the heart from the inside. **This is a picture of Jesus at Jairus's house. Jesus still went to see Jairus's daughter. Jairus was thankful that Jesus still wanted to go.**

Have the children look at heart number 3. **What do you see?** *(people who are sad and crying)* **These people are at the daughter's bedside. They are crying because the girl died.** Have the children flip up the heart from the inside. **This is a picture of Jesus with Jairus's daughter after Jesus reached out his hand and brought the girl back to life. Everyone who knew Jairus and his daughter was very thankful to Jesus. And Jairus and his daughter were especially thankful.**

- **Who was thankful?** *(Jairus, Jairus's daughter, people who knew Jairus and his daughter)*
- **Who do you know that can be thankful?** *(me, you, all of us, everyone)*
- **What are you thankful for?** *(answers will vary)*

Sail Away

Get List:
- Completed *Flippers Up*

Prayer

Have the children each tell one thing they remember from the Bible story. They might look at their *Flippers Up* for reminders. Then have them tell you one thing for which they are thankful. Lead the children in prayer: **Dear God, we love you. We love to learn about you. Thank you for teaching us to be thankful. In Jesus' name, amen.**

Get List:
- None

Cleanup

As the children clean up, have them repeat this phrase each time they pick something up: "When hearts are sad, cry out to Jesus and you'll be glad."

Get List:
- Completed *Flippers Up*
- Construction paper hearts
- Copy of *Home Connection* for each child

Homeward Bound

As the children prepare to leave, make sure they have their completed *Flippers Up* they made for Bible Story Time and a *Home Connection*. Cut out little hearts from the construction paper. Hand a heart to the children as they leave. Tell them this heart reminds you to have a heart full of thanks.

- What does your heart remind you of?
- Who can have a thankful heart?

PINT-SIZE BIBLE BITES

It was against customary rules to touch a dead body. It is very significant that Jesus reached out his hand and touched the hand of the dead girl.

TEACHER TIP

Encourage the children to make thankfulness a habit. Tell them to try to think of three things every day that they are thankful for. Maybe they can keep a thanksgiving list.

Home Connection
Dive In!

Title: A Father's Plea

Bible Story: Luke 8:40–42, 49–56

Bible Truth: Be thankful for all things.

Bible Verse: Devote yourselves to prayer, being watchful and thankful. (Colossians 4:2)

● In this lesson your child **heard** the story of Jairus and how Jesus healed his daughter.

● In this lesson your child **learned** that Jairus called out to Jesus when his daughter was sick and was thankful when she was well.

● In this lesson your child **remembered** that we should have thankful hearts.

In the Bible story, Jairus tried to find Jesus in a crowd. He needed Jesus' immediate attention because his daughter was at home dying. Jairus knew that Jesus was the only one who could help his daughter. Jairus found Jesus, but it seemed too late because he heard news that his daughter had died. Jesus still went to Jairus' house and brought his daughter back to life. Jairus was very thankful. Teach your child that we also should be thankful.

HOME CONNECTIONS

These are items used during the Bible story lesson that might be commonly found in your home. When your child sees or plays with one of the items mentioned below, help make the connection to the Bible story.

   Hearts: Hearts were used throughout most of the activities in this lesson. When you see heart shapes, remind your child that our hearts should be full of thanks.

   Hands: Jesus reached his hand out to the little girl. When working with your hands, tell your child that your hands remind you of how Jesus reached his hand out to Jairus's daughter in the Bible story.

KEEPING CONNECTED

Here are two simple activities that were used in class during the Bible story lesson, A Father's Plea. Use these activities to help your child remember the Bible story lesson.

Heart to Heart

Cut a large heart from poster board. Give your child some bandages. Ask about situations or people who have hurt your child in the past. It could be physical hurts or emotional hurts. Write the hurts on the bandages. Then stick the bandages to the heart. Tape the heart on the wall. Talk about how Jesus can heal all our hurts.

Hands of Prayer

Devote yourselves to prayer, being watchful and thankful. (Colossians 4:2)

Trace your child's hands onto construction paper, then cut out the hands. On each finger, write a word from the Bible memory verse including the reference. Tape the hands together with the words facing out. Repeat the verse aloud using the hands of prayer.

Prayer

Give your child a bandage and discuss times when you've been hurt. Then talk about how you have been thankful to God for how he's taken care of you. Lead your child in this prayer: **Dear God, thank you for the good times and for being with us in the sad times too. Help us to always be thankful. We love you. In Jesus' name, amen.**

TOPIC INDEX

SCRIPTURE INDEX